PRAISE FOR FINDING MALONE

Finding Malone is refreshing, suspenseful, compelling and life-giving. You can't read this true-life story without being changed.
Les Parrott, Ph.D.
#1 New York Times best-selling Author of The Good Fight

"I've known Dennis Mansfield for over fifteen years. He's spoken at our Thrive Conference, taught my children and served faithfully in association with Focus on the Family for a decade. His latest book, Finding Malone, is exceptional. It successfully deals with the father wound in so many of us – by Dennis being vulnerable, open and incredibly practical."
Ray Johnston
Lead Pastor, Bayside Church

"Finding Malone is the story of love and loss. Dennis Mansfield's life-long time as a "love cat" mirrors my belief that all things can be overcome in love – even the deepest of wounds from one's own father. Reconciliation and redemption form the greatest story in life."
Tim Sanders, author of Love Is the Killer App: How To Win Business and Influence Friends

"Finding Malone is the true companion volume to Dennis Mansfield's break-out first book, Beautiful Nate. It's a story of heart-breaking pain and heart-warming forgiveness between a grown man and his father. I encourage families to read this book and embrace it's powerful healing in your own lives."
Raul Labrador, Member of Congress 1st CD Idaho

D1648766

"In Finding Malone, Dennis Mansfield once again demonstrates his ability to weave a tale that is spiritually and emotionally compelling. Seamlessly stepping between generations and families and issues, Finding Malone is one of those rare reads that both drives you onward and forces you to stop and ponder. Finding Malone offers spiraling encounters with love, redemption, honesty and forgiveness that are much like getting better acquainted with a new best friend."
Bodie and Brock Thoene, Best Selling Authors

Dennis Mansfield, through real heartache and trial has learned what it means to embrace the gift of fatherhood. The term "Father" is a God-given one and therefore its full meaning can be understood only in the context of knowing God personally. Dennis knows this God personally and therefore this book is a picture of his journey and a vital message to those who have the privilege of being fathers. Read it well and carefully for it flows out of a real life experience that has driven my friend Dennis to find answers that bring real hope and restoration.
Malcolm Hedding
Executive Director Emeritus of the International Christian Embassy Jerusalem

"Dennis Mansfield stares down past mistreatment and old stereotypes, and in the process remakes his family and his life. An inspiring tale about Christian charity and how a remarkable man changed the world of those he touched."
Walt Minnick
Former Member of Congress,
Idaho's 1ˢᵗ Congressional District

"The eternal topic of fathers and their sons weaves through Denny Mansfield's inspirational and uplifting real-life story of Finding Malone. It is most satisfying that the tale begins, rather than ends, in a catharsis of faith-based forgiveness by the son of the father - who are themselves at the chronological center of four generations of men doing the best they know how by the 'light that God gave them' to know. Finding an old soldier by the name of Malone then just becomes the rally point of a greatly delayed father-son relationship as well as a banner picked up by the newest young generation of servant-leaders in this family".

Les Szabolcsi
Former US Army officer
President, West Point Class of 1978

"Dennis Mansfield is vulnerable, blunt and honest in Finding Malone. It is is the story of forgiveness and reconciliation – of paying tribute when it seems tribute is not warranted. Finding Malone is a story of finding redemption – it is the story of the cross."

Joe White
Founder, Men at the Cross
Kamp Kanakuk

"Finding Malone is not just a story of forgiveness and honor but a story that brings the reader to self-reflection. Dennis tells this story as if he is sitting in your living room and the mercy and forgiveness that we all desire, he tells the reader is available. A great personal story of the freedom we receive when we give to others what we so badly want for ourselves. Thank you Dennis!"

Bonnie Taylor
Minister to women and families
Saddleback Church, Lake Forest, CA

"Dennis Mansfield's second book, Finding Malone, rounds out the story of hope via the story of forgiveness. I've worked with thousands of people over the years who, once they learn to forgive, can then find hope for their lives. Finding Malone provides a clear pathway to forgiving others and gaining hope for yourself."
Wayne McKamie, Founder, Focus Seminars

"Dennis has given a tremendous gift to people in general, men in particular. Through Dennis' authenticity and candor, I was given entrance into an intimate, broken relationship between him and his father. I cringed as Dennis painted the picture of growing up, I held my breath reading of his writing a tribute for his dad and I cried at the results that came from the experience.
Finding Malone is a gift, giving me hope around the area of forgiveness, giving me tools to forgive and giving me a picture of the power that comes from forgiveness. In inviting me to climb up his family tree, Dennis has given me the courage to work on my own. I can wholeheartedly encourage anyone to engage with this book."
Gary L. Gaddini
Lead Pastor, Peninsula Covenant Church,
Redwood City, CA

"Finding Malone, is a story of each of our own fathers and us.
It is an especially powerful example for those who have not had a loving, open and forgiving relationship with their father, but longed for one. "Finding Malone" forced us to reflect on our own relationships with our fathers; we let go of areas of

unforgiveness. This story encouraged us to heal any brokenness in those relationships. It is a book of healing."

Mr. and Mrs. Michael Sollazzo, Esq.,
Capital Planning Advisors, Inc.
Advanced Planning Counsel & Principal

FINDING MALONE

FINDING MALONE

DENNIS MANSFIELD

endurancepress

Visit Endurance Press' website at www.endurancepress.com

Finding Malone

PUBLISHED BY ENDURANCE PRESS

577 N Cardigan Ave

Star, ID 83669 U.S.A.

Cover Photo of Dennis and Bill Mansfield: credit Ken Mansfield

Cover Photo of Mrs. Malone; credit Colin Mansfield

Back cover photo courtesy of A.J. Malone Family.

Author Photo credit Chad Estes, Starry Night Photography.

Interior Photo's credit "Family Photography"

ISBN 978-0-9960146-8-7

eISBN 978-0-9856746-7-0

®2013 Dennis Mansfield

Cover Design by Teal Rose Design Studio's

Printed in the United States of America

First Edition 2013

Contents

*This work is dedicated to the two fathers
I've had in my life and to their wives:*

*William E. Mansfield, after whom I received my
first and seldom-used legal name and from whom I
inherited my first love of movies, barbeque, leadership
and family (you'll understand…) He was one of my
best friends for the last 19 years of his life.*

*Marilyn Mansfield, my stepmother and friend.
You bore the burden of a family torn apart by divorce,
loving your husband and his family as though they
were your own – because eventually they were your
own. Thank you.*

*Lawrence F. Rampenthal, my father-in-law for 35
years, who has continued to show me unconditional
love, sweet friendship and the support that a friend
of the heart always gives. Thanks for allowing me to
marry your second daughter!*

*Vonda Firestone, my mother-in-law, former busi-
ness partner (many moons ago) and my friend. You
have loved your step-kids (and in-laws) as though
they were your own. You have loved all the grandchildren because they were your own. Thank you.*

*Through both couples I learned to shoulder the glo-
rious burden of wearing the painfully wonderful and
yet imperfect title of Father.*

Note from Susan Mansfield

The complete and total healing that I witnessed after Dennis forgave his father was absolutely miraculous.

Out of sheer will and obedience he wrote his tribute to his father. This precipitated a most amazing change of position for both his father and him.

Dennis and I had been married 18 years when this break-through occurred. Until then, Dennis had been deeply angry at his father often expressing his feelings of hatred toward him. He spoke poorly about his Dad and had a great deal of embraced injury inside that could accidently seep out at others, primarily me. He seemed always discontented. Often his anger was accelerated by even the smallest conflict that came about through simply living life.

Dennis desired his father's love and never felt it was given to him. So he sought that love from his next closest emotional tie - me. He wanted me to love him and fill up an ever-empty emotional tank. This was such a burden on me - one I could never fill, no matter how hard I tried. The depth of painful pressure was beyond anything I had ever faced. Nothing I could do was enough to satisfy his dad-deficient hunger.

Wives are not meant to love like fathers.

After the tribute and subsequent forgiveness, almost instantly Dennis was a different person. He gently responded to me rather than harshly reacting at me - with balanced expectations, he was able to move forward through losses without blame. He felt better about himself and saw his father fully for who he was – a flawed man, yet fully capable of loving and being loved.

Dennis Mansfield truly forgave his father, Bill.

Like all of us, Bill Mansfield did the best he could with the tools he had. As a parent of three children I cannot begin to *understand what it took to raise seven little ones. He must have been so stretched and stressed. What he never had in his own life, he could not give to his kids.*

He was an unforgiving man.

Lack of forgiveness hinders one's growth and sets into motion blame for things beyond a peron's scope and influence. The insignificance that subsequently flows from an unforgiving heart destroys other relationships – and ultimately oneself.

For Dennis and me, It was taking such a toll on our marriage.

Once the forgiveness took place, however, Dennis was able to view his father in a clearer, fairer, more accurate light. This caused complete healing not only in his relationship with his father, it also transferred into a healthier marriage for us. Dennis was able to love out of a heart of compassion, thankfulness, and forgiveness.

This single event of forgiveness, between father and son at a Father's Day family barbeque dinner, was a full and complete turning point in their lives and in mine.

It captured the very aroma of life in a moment's notice, forever substituting fragrance for odor.

How thankful I am to have a husband who was willing to fulfill a simple request by his wife – thus initiating the obedient work of forgiving his father. Though my father-in-law reaped the benefit of finally knowing his son, I too profited from their healing for the rest of my life.

Today Dennis is fulfilled as a husband - knowingly and willingly receiving the kind of love only I am able to give him, a much different type of love and respect than he could ever have received from his father. Dennis is a man contented.

Susan Mansfield, Feb. 22, 2013

Scripture:

3 Praise be to the God and Father of our Lord Jesus Christ, the Father of compassion and the God of all comfort, 4 who comforts us in all our troubles, so that we can comfort those in any trouble with the comfort we ourselves receive from God.

5 For just as we share abundantly in the sufferings of Christ, so also our comfort abounds through Christ. 6 If we are distressed, it is for your comfort and salvation; if we are comforted, it is for your comfort, which produces in you patient endurance of the same sufferings we suffer.

7 And our hope for you is firm, because we know that just as you share in our sufferings, so also you share in our comfort.

II Corinthians 1:3-7 New International Version of the Bible

TRIBUTE
and
HONOR

Chapter 1
Facing the pain

I didn't quite hear it, *did I?*

Maybe I didn't *want* to hear it.

But she was speaking on the phone to someone familiar.

"You're coming through town in a week and a half, headed to a class reunion? You need a place to stay one night?"

I motioned to my bride as she held the receiver in her hand, I pantomimed the logical question, "Who are you talking to?", mentally processing through the list of possible out-of-state friends who would be old enough for a 15 or 20 year class reunion.

The year was 1995. My bride and I were both 39 years old at the time and had been married for 18 years; we were the parents of three kids.

She dismissed me with a slight wave of her hand,

turning away from me and continuing the conversation. "*Sure,* we have plenty of room, we'd *love* to have you overnight."

I furrowed my brow as I looked at her, saying, "Plenty of room? *No we don't! Who* are you talking to?" Definitely out-of-staters, but which state? How many of them? I was just full of questions and semi-surly comments.

We lived in a modest 3-bedroom 1600 square foot home, barely big enough for our growing family of two young boys, Nathan and Colin and a daughter in between them, Megan.

My bride, Susan, concluded her phone conversation by saying, "Oh Den and the kids will *love* seeing you. You bet! See ya in a few days!"

As Susan, coyly placed the receiver back on the phone set, I could tell she was somewhat hesitant, knowing that what she was about to tell me would be distressing.

She looked at the ground and then breathed deeply, "Well… that was your Dad. He and your step-mom need a place to stay as they make their way to his 50th high school class reunion. I said they could stay with us."

My dad?

There it was. Not a friend from college or a high school buddy who wanted to stop by. Nope. Not a friend at all. *My dad.*

The decision had unilaterally been made to allow the person I hated the most in my life to use my precious home as a motel on his way to a class reunion.

It made me ill.

And it made me furious — both at my father for asking to stay with us and at my wife for answering yes.

You see, I held nothing in my heart for my dad but contempt.

Nothing.

Too hard to read?

Maybe for some.

Too hard to write?

Not for me.

My father, William E. Mansfield, served in the US armed forces at the end of WWII, throughout Korea and during the early years of Vietnam. His clear success in uniform stood in contrast to his deep difficulty in relating to those he loved, along with his failed aspirations as a husband and father. In joining the ranks of the millions of servicemen who saved the free world from tyranny, he became a tyrant to the ones he loved.

He initiated pain through power, tried to control those under him by fear; yet, he sought desperately to receive the accolades of those under whom he served. He *loved* his career and unsuccessfully attempted to *like* his family. He was a man in search of honor and hope, caring little for requesting forgiveness of others.

He failed to be a student of his own family's expressions of love. With seven, and then later, nine children the entire family's requests for love seemed to be a cacophony of noise to his mind. It was as if he put his hands over his ears, refusing to hear — or not having the bandwidth to comprehend the pain he had caused. Broken hearts were felt everywhere in his family. Babies were acceptable to him, he just didn't like kids, it seemed.

As little kids, the seven children of Bill Mansfield saw it. He'd treat us so poorly, belittling each child, beating some, slapping others. Disrespectfully snapping his fingers towards the backseat of the family car as he drove. This was often followed by wildly flailing that same free hand, slapping whatever it came in contact with. Such was the mean-spirited and violent fathering of Sgt. Bill Mansfield.

That's how we traveled.

Once we'd arrive in our family automobile at any of our destinations, he'd have us line up by age like "stair steps" and march cutely in with him — looking like the perfect *Sound of Music* family. More often than not, the adults that met us would coo and smile at how beautiful we all looked and acted.

Acted.

As kids, we saw the hypocrisy of this successful man at work who came home as an unsuccessful father.

No one can completely hide their real self from their kids, can they? I saw how disrespectfully he treated my mom, too. He was mean, cutting and mocking of her my entire childhood. I have no memory of them even exchanging a kiss in front of me, though I am sure they did in the early years.

They dated during the war and married just twenty-four months after the end of WWII. She was a beautiful and skilled sergeant in the Marine Corps during the war. He was a handsome sailor, two years her junior. She outranked him, much to his concern. They met in the lusty wartime of Washington DC and fell in love.

His love apparently had time constraints and conditions.

And this is how he treated her after seven children and twenty years. In a sad sort of way, he was non-selective in his vitriol and pain. He caused his family to hate him; in time, this included his wife.

Those family memories of deep anger and pain often flooded my mind. They seemed always present; at that very moment, even. As an adult I was being asked by my bride to invite this man into my house so that he could impact my own children, *if even only for a day and a night.*

I paused, looked at Susan after she had informed me of her one-sided hospitality decision and then convulsively spit the words out of my mouth, "you have got to be kidding me. What is this some sick joke? I can't believe it!" I yelled.

I turned from her and felt I *had* to walk away — my anger was white hot. Then I heard her speak, slowly and clearly. Forcefully and yet kindly she said, "No. It's not a joke. It's a chance for you to grow up, a chance for you to live your faith out loud. Your kids hear everyday from you about your faith in God and Jesus. But acting this way makes you as big a hypocrite as he."

I pivoted on the toe of my right shoe and swiveled directly into her line-of-sight, turned to her and saw her steel blue eyes focusing on me. She was unmoved, standing firm.

So I would have to be the person who would move.

I slowly walked back toward her, with a question on my lips, "Why, why would you say such a thing to me? *Grow up?* I *hate* my father. You have no idea how badly he hurt me — my bothers and sisters, my mom." I was now *slow-burn* furious.

Susan answered, "*Why would I say that?* Because it's true". Her look of ironclad confidence and honesty was offsetting to me. Something was happening here at this very moment and I was no longer in control of my house, my wife or my comfortable anger towards my father. This was some type of high impact God moment — *if I'd allow it to be.*

She continued, "You've carried a deep hatred for your father since the time I met you, 18 years ago. It's affected you, your life and me. I believe it may terribly torture you into your future... into *our* future."

She hit me the hardest with this, "And how you treat your father is teaching your kids how they should treat you! You are poisoning your own well and you refuse to do anything except force your family to drink from it!"

I've been hit before. In Beast Barracks basic training at the United States Military Academy, my company commander at West Point was brutal. When I first served in politics, I served as press secretary to a former Green Beret, then running for US Congress. He was brutal to a young man wanting to make his name in politics. There were many more before them: uncaring coaches and sarcastic teachers in grade school and in church.

The prize in the past, however, went to my father. My dad said some of the *most* brutal things to me that I'd ever heard in my life.

But this was the hardest hit I had *yet* received - because Susan loved me — deeply loved me and I was certain that my father had never loved me.

I was teaching my kids to hate me, as I hated my own father?

I unintentionally fell backwards into a nearby chair. It was as if I just lost control and the chair caught me.

Slowly I said to Susan, "That hurts worse than anything you could have ever said to me".

In the deepest regions of my soul, I felt a pain that I had long-ago thought I had eluded — one that was now directed at me from my wife instead of my father.

I didn't want to look at her, I wanted to hate her because she was wrong but I could not.

I also wanted to hate her because she was right.

Susan then said to me in a loving, tender voice, "It doesn't have to be this way about your dad. You can overcome the years of hatred you hold for your dad. You may not believe me but there is a way, I'm telling you upfront that my way doesn't seem to make sense at first... but it will work."

She had my attention.

"Go on..." I almost inaudibly said.

"Den, do you remember when my mom turned 50? I had been reading a book by Dennis Rainey. Its title is "The Tribute". In it he writes of coming to grips with the folks who most love us and who most hurt us... normally our family members fill both those slots... most often our fathers and mothers. Then in the book he suggests writing them a formal letter — a *tribute* of sorts. You know my mom and I always had a great friendship; I realized that I needed to honor her for all the things she did that were right. Remember? And I wrote that one-page tribute to her and read it out loud at her party."

I was sort of sideswiped. Yes, I fully remembered the wonderful tribute that Susan had written and then had spoken to her mother, Wanda, at that event, a few years before. It was beautiful. Susan loved her mom deeply. They had a deeply fun friendship, full of laughter and respect.

Many years later, when her father, Larry, turned 80, she gave him a similarly written honor and tribute. Larry Rampenthal is a hard-working man who saw his own 18-year long marriage collapse through divorce, when my bride was a young girl. Yet, he was never absent from his kids' lives, he met his monthly child support payments for his large brood, which was no small feat. Larry was the kind of father and, *I soon came to understand,* father-in-law that understood honor because he practiced it everyday.

A letter to people like that made sense to me.

But to my dad? Writing such a letter made no sense. None at all. Write a tender, compassionate tribute to a man that I wished I have never known, let alone wished had never been my father? I was stunned to silence until like a volcanic eruption I stood up and convulsively blurted into her face: "What are you on, crack?"

Silence met me in return.

Susan would not back down, "It's easy to love the ones who love *you*, Den. We all do that. Yeah, I am blessed to have a mom and dad whom I love. But that's not the point. It's no mistake that your dad was your dad. God didn't do right by me and then blow it with you. He knew you would be Bill Mansfield's son and He's waiting on you to wake up and realize it."

I slumped over the back of the overstuffed sofa chair. My passive response fueled her strength to go on. She picked up a yellow pad and some pens. "I want you to take these pens and paper and go into our master bedroom, kneel down and ask God to show you what to write — I want you to write a tribute to your dad — for *your* sake, if not for *his*! It is time to be set free from the handcuffs of hatred, Den."

At first I stood there unmoved.

Then, I slowly turned in response and stretched out to my full six-foot stature, grabbed the tools of this *foolish* exercise from her and looked at all five feet three inches of my then-38 year old wife. "Ok, great…I'll do this stupid little thing for you, but realize this — that I'm only gonna be able to write something like 'Thanks for not killing me when you beat the hell out of me as a kid. Thanks for teaching me the power of hating people.' This thing you are asking me to do is an effort in futility. It's going to take me hours — watch and see." I walked up the staircase to our second floor and then into our bedroom with the almost-expected thud-thud-thud of a man headed to his own execution.

I slammed the door, placed the yellow pad and multi-colored pens on the beautiful handcrafted bedspread that covered our king-size bed.

I then slowly knelt down to pray.

Clasping my hands together, in a whisper I prayed a desperate prayer "God what is this, a cosmic joke? I hate that man. I hate everything about him. There is nothing I have that's a good memory of him, nor any attribute from my father that is good. *Nothing.*"

Then there was silence.

But not for too long.

I heard God's voice say to my spirit. "Nothing?"

I was more than a bit surprised. I wondered if I should even answer.

"Lord is that you?"

"Nothing?" He replied. "Really?"

I'd never had this happen in the 15 or so years that I'd been a Christian. I'd heard others say that the Lord "speaks" to them... but that always happened to other people, not me. Normally I'd read about it in books or heard third-party stories at some overly dramatic church service somewhere. But that wasn't *my* church.

However, I was in *my* house, *my* bedroom, hearing God's voice ask me two one-word questions.

"Nothing?"

"Really?"

I knew it was He because there was no way I would have posed those questions to myself. I KNEW my dad. I KNEW what he had failed to do. I KNEW there was nothing of any value that he had imparted to me. No gift, no attribute.

What I apparently didn't KNOW was that God was moving into my neighborhood with me to ask me two profoundly simple questions.

And he was talking directly to me.

Nothing? I repeated to myself and was sure of it.

But this response jarred me.

I picked up a common everyday cheap blue ink pen and *woodenly* placed the tip of the ballpoint pen on the first line of the lined yellow page.

What happened next was remarkable, even after all these years that I experienced it.

The pen in my right hand began to move.

I could feel my finger muscles holding the pen. I could see the initial movement of the very normal blue ink pen move in such a very abnormal fashion across a yellow page. A word appeared. Then another. It became a list of words.

I was seeing my hand write the words; more than that I was acknowledging the words on the list as true. "Movies. BBQ. Leadership." On and on the words rolled... out from under the obedient placement of pen on paper.

I slowly became an active participant. I thought of other words, placed them on the growing list. I wrote full sentences and connected some dots. I saw a picture appear before my eyes of the many things that my father had done with me and for me.

And before I could count the minutes that I had invested — for somehow time had changed course and was no longer dependent on the arms of the nearby clock — I was finished.

I stood up from the side of the bed where I had been kneeling and as I walked through the master bedroom doorway, I was like a man who had witnessed an angelic visitation. But my name wasn't George Bailey and there was no Clarence, with the rank of Angel, Second Class.

I had witnessed, first-hand, the presence and power of the Holy Spirit.

I looked like it, too.

Susan saw me exit out of our bedroom and walked over to me as if to ask me if I was either in need of something else from her to complete the task OR whether I had given up on even attempting it — for it had only been a few minutes.

Then she looked at my face.

She saw in my facial features that something else had happened. I simply extended my left arm and held out the yellow pad for her - as a deaf man would. I had no words. She received back the pad, now with the writing on it, she walked downstairs to that same sofa couch to plop into it, as I had earlier done.

She read the words I had written.

Then Susan slowly looked up and with surprise in her eyes, said "This is beautiful, Den. Beautiful."

I knew that what was written was true, but I played such a little part in preparing what they meant.

I knew that almost all of it was from a God-breathed memory that had previously and purposefully failed to allow it even surface as a vague childhood memory.

Here it was, *the tribute.*

My dad was just days away and I would now have to do something even more painful than quietly write it.

I'd have to read it out loud to him.

And I really did *not* look forward to his response. His past history showed that nothing good came of my family or me being vulnerable around him. Especially after how for years, *before they were divorced*, I had seen him treat my mom so poorly whenever she tried to do something special for him or by being vulnerable around him.

He was brutal.

She became a woman worn down by a personal war.

But she wasn't always that way.

Chapter 2

War and an Irishman's daughter

Virginia Agnes Maguire Mansfield was a beautiful girl, when she was young. Pictures of her as a thin and stunning Marine Corps clerk in WWII show pride, confidence and beauty.

She was elegant, yet at the same time a tad awkward — as though she really didn't believe she was as beautiful as everyone said.

She came from tough Irish stock. "Ginny" was born in 1925 to an Irishman, John Joseph Maguire, and his bride, Etta Viola Cramer, of strong German background. The clan was *almost* Irish through and through. She was second of six — all with *"Jesus, Mary and Joseph"* Irish names.

Mom graduated from high school right smack in the middle of WWII. Her father and mother loved and cared for her and their other kids in a fiercely mystically Irish way. The world of "Joe" Maguire and his large family in the 1940's was a comfortably safe world.

And it was a successful one. He had homes when other people barely had a single house. He traveled and summered at Ocean City, New Jersey. Six kids, a respectable reputation and career and enough money to be comfortable.

But it had not always been that way. He'd been born in 1895. He learned how to fight when he was a young man. He came of age during that first decade of the new 20th century, running on the cobble stoned streets of Philadelphia - the midwife-city to our nation's founding.

Joe Maguire, was a tough son of a gun. Born tough.

He was an Irish street thug from South Philly. Short of stature, Joe not only knew how to fight but how to win. Stories echoed through the years within my family of his hard edge and his even harder fists. Being Irish in Philly at the turn of the 19th and the beginning of the 20th centuries was not an easy nationality to have.

Joe's father and mother immigrated directly from Ireland to Philadelphia and took jobs where they could. An Irishman's Catholic religion followed them all the way to the cradle of American Independence. Joe's parents knew that they could work hard. And they could worship their God hard. It was something they were used to — something that brought both lands together if only for an hour each week during Catholic mass, as if the Atlantic Ocean didn't exist. At least on Sundays.

On Mondays, the differences were far clearer.

Joe was Roman Catholic, hard as nails and unwilling to let another man have his way with him, with his family or with his friends. Day after day, month after month, he was on the defensive. By 10 years of age, however, Joe showed something different than many of the other boys with whom he ran. He knew how to make money fast and how to keep it. Joe liked money. It was a great equalizer in a world of rampant bigotry against Irish Catholics.

He loved to read. He read about President Teddy Roosevelt and Europe. He read about Kaisers and economists. He read about money.

He also developed a love for writing. The knuckles that pounded out payment of a past-due penny from another Irish urchin could also hold firmly a fountain pen pressed to cotton stock paper, writing down his thoughts. His math abilities began to show themselves too.

By his teen years he knew everybody there was to know in South Philly; and he knew everything he needed to know about each person. He ran hard, fought harder and made money most of all.

But money can't stop medical problems.

Young Joe caught a severe cold in his teen years and it settled as an infection near his left mastoid bone, just behind his ear lobe. At the time very little was known about how to deal with certain infections. The doctors decided to drill into his skull, into the very mastoid bone to relieve pressure and attempt to drain the infection. It was a gamble. He would have a permanent hole, the size of a half-inch drill bit, whether it worked or not.

The hole went deep, but the infection went deeper. When he awoke from the operation, he could no longer hear in his left ear. The hole would be life-long proof to him of a medical community that *practiced* medicine on its patients. Practice paid off for others when it came to medicine, but not for Joe. He would be deaf in that ear for the rest of his life.

At this key juncture in Joe Maguire's young adult life, he realized that a lot more money could be made by businesses than by bravado and bullying. As if surrounded by an epiphany of bright lights, Joe looked up from his streets and saw the businesses that lined those streets — successful businesses. The most successful in Philadelphia were insurance businesses — life, property and casualty insurance firms.

So it was that the son of an Irish immigrant went from the often rainy and rough streets of South Philly into the warm and professional downtown offices of moneyed businessmen; scions of Ben Franklin's wealth, sons of geld, the honored young men who knew how to make money and save most of it.

Joe opened the door of that world and let himself in.

And this young businessman's dreams of wealth soared. The budding insurance business seemed to be something that a hard working hustler from the streets could do. Joe was smart, understood the mentoring, was affable and could close a sale.

He made money and he made a reputation for himself. By the end of his professional career he had become President of the Insurance Agents and Brokers of Philadelphia, Chairman of the Property Committee for the State of Pennsylvania, Chairman of the Eastern Agents Conference Committee of the National Association of Agents and Broker.

It all started when he wanted to get out of the streets of South Philly.

In 1917 the nation was impacted by a war to end all wars — WWI - a European war being fought in French trenches with German bullets and British helmets — doughboy helmets — the kind that protected their wearers from shrapnel that rained down directly from above.

The helmets became *American* helmets when Woodrow Wilson entered the nation into war. Styled after their British cousins' helmets, the chinstraps were leathery and canvas, connected by small black hook links, fastened from the soldier-wearer's left to right. They were upside-down bouncing buckets of steel, making the soldiers and sailors feel as though, *while fighting*, that they were also in some bizarre head-and-neck balancing routine. Yes, they saved lives; but did security of the helmets warrant the painful wearing of these clumsy things?

America's eastern coast made millions of these helmets. Some 5 million were issued to soldiers, Marines and sailors who enlisted in the US Armed Forces during WWI. As in any war, the suppliers over-stocked the shelves. Millions of helmets went to war. The rest waited in warehouses that lined streets in Philly, Washington DC, New York City and other large cities. Such were huge cavernous halls of neatly folded burlap olive-drab uniforms, leather pouches for various purposes, backpacks and night rolls. And awkwardly stacked above the boxes were the helmets - stacked and restacked, placed neatly, if hesitantly, on wooden pallets and tightly anchored down by thin but effective canvas straps - for quick shipment to the distant front, if needed.

Joe Maguire could not wear such a uniform. His local board refused him. Seems the world at war didn't want a young Irishman *already with a hole in his head.* How ironic it became to Joe that the very thing he could do well with his fists was somehow now being withheld from him. He was a warrior without a war.

So he made money instead. Lots of it.

He supported the war effort every day he went to work.

With soldiers rushing off to war, death notices soon followed. Insurance became a much needed but an undesired item for wives and mothers, fathers and friends to purchase for their Yanks that were going 'over there'. Though few said it, many realized that some would *not* be coming home.

The insurance business boomed and Joe Maguire was there to help make that boom even bigger. He did it well. And he did it quickly. A good businessman never really knows when demand will drop. Timing is essential. Good timing is even more so. Winning is everything. To be on the wrong end of a bad business deal is to lose, big time.

So, Joe stayed on the correct side of business deals - forcefully, and with an eye on the world conflict's possible resolution. He sold as much insurance as he could; he needed to own an insurance company, if he could.

The war *was* resolved on a blustery mid-November day in 1918. Peace arrived — and yet fear failed to depart.

It had good reason not to. The armistice was tenuous. The vanquished Germanic soldiers of Imperial Germany were not so willing to go quietly into the western front's sunset. Their brokenness and fear forced them back across the Rhine River to their families and their homes.

Fear also came home with the American soldiers.

Husbands came home. Worn uniforms were taken off for the last time. Swords were hammered into plowshares.

Except for those lonely brigades of unused burlap uniforms that lay neatly folded on industrial areas and dirty streets that bordered them. Precisely stacked and purposely placed in deep wooden crates, military uniforms were suddenly a thing of the past.

Equipment was also a part of that story. Brand new and unused backpacks and shoulder straps were thrown into large sized crates along with helmets and chinstraps, weapons and bayonets. Uniform crate after uniform crate, packed with the essentials of personal war protection: woven jackets and pleated pants, olive drab woolen shirts and iron dough-boy helmets — always the helmets. Heavy and cumbersome, awkward and unneeded, the younger Irishmen who worked the warehouses moved these unruly heavy boxed assortments into a uniform fashion of uniform order - to the back of the warehouse. Never to be needed again, it seemed.

While he roared through the remainder of the war, Joe eventually met and married Viola in 1918, growing his insurance business as they grew their family. One child, one major client, three children, more east coast business, six Irish lads and lassies — leadership in Insurance associations and increased wealth. Somewhere along the line, Joe became comfortable with laughter — he held the laughter of wealthy men who no longer needed to be financially frightened. Like all things he tried, he did well at being wealthy. His sardonic humor began to seem as comfortable to him as did the lifestyle that wealth gave him.

Comfortable. That was how he felt. *Comfortable.*

His second child was his first daughter. They named her Virginia Agnes Maguire — after a family friend, a nun who was named *Aggie Pat*. The kids used to laugh and guess who they were named after, as they all grew up and reviewed their possible namesakes. No one knew a Virginia in the family and though they loved the namesake no one really liked the actual name "Agnes", least of whom was Ginny. She was thin, beautiful and funny from the start. She seemed to hold her father's heart, as well. Other children came along to the Maguire clan in the twenties and early thirties, but Ginny was always her father's first sweet daughter.

By the late 1930's, the kids became teenagers. As the calendar pages turned to 1940, the distant war cries echoed closer to home, daily they seemed to jump off the front-page of the Philadelphia Enquirer. Odd words suddenly became quickly familiar. *Berlin. Poland. Fuehrer. Lend/Lease. Fascist. Nazi. World War II.*

Joe Maguire held his breath. His first two kids were just old enough to enlist in the service. With all his might the warrior wanted to go in place of his kids, if he could. But his age and his ear would not allow it.

His kids went, anyway. First Jack, then with no warning, Ginny. The male namesake went to the Marines and eventually to Guadalcanal, the beautiful young lady joined him in the Marines, but her tour of duty was Washington D.C. No other siblings followed, as their young ages would not permit it.

When Ginny finished boot camp, her orders for DC

came. She stopped by to see her father, walking down the side streets of South Philly, past the warehouses that had held the previously "unneeded" uniforms from what was now being called World War I.

Those crates had been relocated to cities like Boston and New York a few years earlier - prior to December 7th 1941 - and handed out to soldiers, sailors and Marines who had joined the American "peace-time military".

What other uniforms were they to wear? Especially the helmets.

Time marched on.

Ginny took her place in the nation's capital, living at an all female barracks within the district, working for the Marine Corps providing clerical duties, doing her best to help the war effort. It was 1943 and WWII was well under way.

A chance visit with a girlfriend to a dance at the enlisted man's Marine Corps and Navy one Friday night changed her life. A beautifully handsome sailor in his neatly pressed dress blue "crackerjack" uniform, holding in his hands his pristine cap anxiously rolled up, approached the two beautiful female Marines.

"Would you like to dance, miss?" asked the sailor.

And Ginny quickly said "yes!". The sailor looked a bit embarrassed and then took her hand as they walked out on the dance floor to dance to Juke Box Saturday Night.

It was an ominous beginning for these two young people who would become my parents.

Ominous because he had asked the *other* young lady to dance, not Ginny. The woman who would become my mother hadn't noticed.

Their romance blossomed *anyway.*

The year was 1947 and Bill Mansfield went to Ocean City, New Jersey to ask Joe Maguire for his daughter's hand. Mom was 22 and a Marine — she hardly needed this young suitor to knock at the family's summer beach home for acceptance.

But her father Joe needed to hear the knock and answer the door.

The two men shook hands, eyed each other and then sat down to dinner. The Maguire clan engulfed them. Ginny's siblings hunkered down to see who this man was, who wanted to become a part of their sprawling family. Young Walt, Muriel, Eddie, and Dick wiggled in their seats and listened.

Joe knew how to read a man. He'd done it his whole life. This was going to be his most thorough reading of a man yet. *It had to be.* This was his first daughter. The family's first wedding.

There's no family history written down describing how that meeting went, but my guess is that it didn't go well for a first meeting. Joe had known men like Bill Mansfield his whole life. They were hot-shots, arrogant men who thought more highly of themselves then they should have.

Spit and polish? Maybe, but more than likely he was more polish than spit. Guys like this young suitor tended to achieve success by personality, not character and hard work.

The fact that Bill wasn't Catholic loomed as a greater obstacle than anything to the Maguire clan.

Joe didn't like it. Another way to say it was, Joe didn't like *him*.

But Ginny did. A lot. Her dad's eyes saw this.

The approval, therefore, was given to Ginny to be married to this "damn protestant". It was suggested that in time the young man should convert to her faith, placing a seed in his mind that would later come to fruition in Korea, a few war years later.

The wedding was planned for early August, 1947. It would NOT be a church wedding but rather a wedding in the priest's rectory. That was final. The groom wasn't a Catholic. That was Joe Maguire.

Then somewhere in the mix of time and events, of planning and thinking, something went wrong. Family legend tends to link it to the ring Bill gave Ginny — that it was from a previous fiancée. But, there was most certainly more to the story. Bill was an unforgiving sort, even when the ring he offered his rebound-bride was the same one that had been returned to him in a Dear John letter. Forgiveness was not his long suit.

Ginny called off the wedding with Bill and a furious and embarrassed Seaman Bill Mansfield left in a tirade as the taxi picked him up. The train station awaited him along with an uncertain future in the Navy.

Joe Maguire could feel this in his bones. His daughter didn't need this showboat, he felt. *Good riddance!*

Then, in a fit of second-guessing and much to Joe's chagrin, Ginny enlisted the driving skills of a younger brother, and they sped down to the train tracks, in hopes of stopping the premature ending of this love story.

Like a scene from a Frank Capra film of the 40's the fiancés were reunited on the platform after the bride-to-be begged the would-be groom to exit the train. Bill never understood the need to ask for forgiveness from her, though it seemed he easily accepted Ginny's apology. They were married days later.

Their 27-year-long marriage would show they never understood that there is a world of difference between issuing an apology and initiating an act of forgiveness.

An apology is a one-sided statement at someone who has been hurt or injured, by another individual

- through word or deed. It's not uncommon to see an apology given because of small social infractions, as when someone accidentally steps on your toe in an elevator, "Sorry *if* that hurt, dear." As well, the politician arrested for drunk driving tends to issue an apology, "if I injured anyone, I apologize" tends to be the line in the script.

It's all one-sided, passive voice and in the end fairly useless.

A request to be forgiven is a whole other thing. It requires that the two parties involved in a problem interact. Forgiveness is initiated in the active voice. "I blew it last evening, sweetheart; will you forgive me for what I did?" And then the offended party has the opportunity of forgiving the culprit or not.

Once forgiveness is requested, it's up to the offended party to respond. This is a two-sided event.

Putting it a different way, an apology is like a monolog. A request for forgiveness is like a dialog.

Time eventually passed but, the family in which I grew up never understood the drastic differences between these two concepts.

I could see the needed difference clearly in my parent's ongoing destructive actions against each other and their children, but could I see it in myself?

I was about to find out.

Chapter 3

Tribute to Bill Mansfield

O ur modest two-story 1600 square foot home of 3 bedrooms had a front room as you entered the house and as well as a little TV room off the kitchen, near the back of the home.

It wasn't a tract home, but it *was* a spec home built by an enterprising independent contractor.

The lot was an odd pie-shaped parcel of property with our house set back on a cul-de-sac and all the kids of the local neighborhoods loved living in that vicinity. We'd been living there for over two years.

When we transplanted from Southern California to Idaho in 1991, we decided to rent first, wherever we could, so that later as we became more familiar with Boise, we would learn where we could find a nice neighborhood and buy a home. This was a nice neighborhood. We bought a nice home!

Our three kids really loved this home.

One of the things we all loved about the house's floor plan was the position of the formal dining room. We brought a fairly large formal cherry wood dining table up with us from California and wanted a place to display it, while using it on a daily basis. Functional and yet beautiful — that was our goal.

That dinner table lay parallel against the northern-most wall. The wall's large picture window was just a little higher than the level of the table line and delivered the days' beauty; it framed the four seasons, which are such a part of the Idaho way of life.

The day that my father and stepmother showed up to have their motel sleepover prior to his high school class reunion held a particularly strange beauty for those who had eyes to see. It was Sunday June 10th.

Ironically, the calendar said it was Father's Day 1995.

Father's Day?

God's sense of humor was skillfully killing me. Strange at times, but wonderful, nonetheless.

There at the end of that gorgeous cherry wood table sat my 67-year-old father, William E. Mansfield and my step mom, Marilyn Mansfield. The table was set for my whole young family of five and the two of them, featuring a sumptuous BBQ feast.

Before I continue, allow me first to go back a step - to that list of beneficial attributes I observed about my father and had, *ever so hesitantly,* written down at my bride's cajoling — and the Lord's audible prompting.

Top among the items on my Heaven-sent list was that my dad loved to take me to the movies. Ever since I was a little child, dad would take those of us among my siblings who were old enough, to go see a film on whatever Air Force Base we were stationed. We loved seeing films!

Next, I remembered and wrote down the memories of Dad's barbecues — smoky and tasty, simmering and lazy. Sweet homemade barbecue & beer sauces that made the beef fall off the bone. His were simply the best barbecues I'd ever tasted.

And right under those two top-drawer items were the next two: travel and leadership. I learned how to lead people by watching his direct approach, coupled with a slight touch of diplomacy and the occasionally needed face-splash of cold water. If he saw that it was needed, he'd willingly deliver. Regarding travel, I most likely had a passport when I was a toddler and have raised my own little kids to travel the world — which all have done.

Four things of great joy lead the way on the list of many other items that duly impacted my life — and yet were left abandoned to the memory of a hurt child within a hurting adult.

That very afternoon, we had attended a showing of the just-released film, "Braveheart", after which my dad sat weeping as the credits rolled by. My son, Nate, and I were on either side of him as he openly cried. Through his sobs we could barely make out the whispery words of the question he asked himself, "Where are all the men who would die for their families and nation?" Nate and I exchanged quizzical looks through wrinkled brows, wondering what this meant.

On our way home from the film, Dad relaxed, wiped away his tears and decided to have us stop at the local supermarket so he could buy a large slab of beef ribs for him to barbecue that night.

The Lord was showing me that the very tribute I was about to deliver to my dad had a clearly spiritual component to it that my bride was completely clued in to.

I smiled the awkward smile of a disbelieving man caught in the center of a miracle.

And the barbecue was indeed sumptuous.

Dad said to me as we sat at the table, "Den why don't you say a little prayer for dinner?"

I found myself looking at him with a tilted head. Saying nothing, I thought to myself, "Thanks for directing me to do something I do EVERY meal—and *then thanks, too, for* dismissing it as a *diminutive* task, *you jerk!*"

But instead, I looked across the nicely set, well-supplied dinner table directly at my father and stated simply, "Dad, before I pray, I'd like to read something that I wrote to you, something that Susan suggested, that Meg calligraphied and that Nate framed. It's a tribute to you."

Then I quickly put the frame up in front of my line-of-sight, blocking all possible visual contact with him so I did not have to see his reactions.

I began to read it out loud, almost mechanically, at first.

My father listened, so did my kids. This is what I read to my dad as a tribute.

"Tribute to Dad"

First memories of
a presidential motorcade
and little boy's eyes peeping over
a church pew
along with Germany, Texas, Michigan
and California.

Brothers, sisters, cars, church, U.S.
Air Force bases,
and lots of Christmas presents,
Hard times, tough times, fun times,
made me who I am
All these things gave me memories.

None of these things gave me character...
You provided that for me.
I honor you today for having

done the best you could with what
you had.

Somewhere in that mix
of all those things
You provided order and direction,
for that I thank you.

The tribute I give is
Really found in the lives of
my children and soon, grandchildren.
You gave me, I give to them
God gave to both of us

Be of good cheer, just as
God overcame the world, He also
overcame the distance between us
For that I thank Him.
It's great to be your son.

June 10, '95   William Dennis Mansfield

When I was done I slowly lowered the frame down
that had blocked my vision of my dad's face. I looked
to him at the head of the table.

But he was not there. His seat was empty! He was
gone.

Though, not too far.

He apparently removed himself from his seat, as I completed my narration, and without me seeing him, quietly walked up and stood right next to me.

Like the butler in the Adam Sandler film *Mr. Deeds,* my dad quickly crept without my detection directly to my right side. It spooked me as I suddenly saw him standing next to me. Not knowing why he was there the thought momentarily flickered by my mind, as though I was 9 years old again, "protect yourself, if he throws a punch."

But he didn't. He couldn't.

Tears had filled his eyes, He couldn't see, he could barely speak.

He reached over to my face, gently cupping it in his hands and kissed me on the lips.

I was in shock. It was now my turn to be the one who could not speak, who could almost not breathe.

Dad slowly gained his voice and began hesitantly apologizing for a litany of disrespectful things he had done to me as a little boy and young man, under his care — dishonoring a kindergarten-me when I asked him to stop smoking by blowing smoke in my face, never being there for the junior high school-version of me with sporting, blowing off events and class activities to the high school version of me, mocking me and belittling the adult me. Most of these things I could barely recall, if at all. But he had recalled them and obviously replayed them over and over again.

I simply stood with my eyes beyond wide-open. Unbelieving. Believing. I was too much in shock to cry. Even as I write these words, I mist up remembering the impossible, recalling the never-to-be, that was.

Now it was *my* time to understand the difference between an apology and an act of forgiveness. It was clear that my dad was doing the best he could with what he had; he was apologizing to me in tears.

And then it was my time to do what I knew I should do.

I forgave him. I spoke these words to the man who most hurt me in my life: "I forgive you, Dad."

Though he did not even know to ask for my forgiveness, I knew I had to extend it. I forgave him for myself, just as my bride said I should.

I forgave my father for all that he had just stated as well as all that I could remember. I also forgave him for what neither of us could recall.

There is no other way to say this next sentence.

Something broke in the Heavens between my dad and me.

Something was severed in eternity that had previously held me in bondage, holding my dad as well, to my sheer amazement. In an instant, in a twinkling of an eye, my pain was over.

I looked at my dad and, for the first time as an adult, said the words that I fully meant, "I love you, Dad." He hugged me and told me he loved me as well.

I had no thought about what would or should come next between us.

When honor is given to those who hurt us, when forgiveness is extended to those whom we hate, miraculous things happen to us. God quickly pours hope and love into us while hatred dies.

I was only there in the moment. The forever-present moment.

I finally realized why God called Himself, "I am".

For all things of the Lord are held loosely by Him in the present.

And we are not to live by our own tightly held fears and hurts...from the past.

It is from that very past that we may have to forgive someone else: ourselves.

Chapter 4

Soldiers and others:
Malone and Mansfield

Anthony J. Malone was from Middletown, CT.

He was a rare breed — a soldier who joined the US Army *between* the wars.

When he joined the Army in 1938, they opened up old wooden dusty crates from two decades earlier and handed out gear. He was issued WWI pants, new-old woolen shirts, dull-shiny doughboy boots and a pristine "old Army" helmet that looked more British than American. Soldiers wore the uniform style their uncles and older brothers had worn during WWI. In particular was that helmet! In it Tony Malone penned his first two initials and then his last name. The leather headgear now bore the markings *"A.J. Malone, Co 'H' 16th med. Reg't, Ford Devens, Mass."*

His post was Fort Devens, Massachusetts and he was trained to be a medic.

Tony Malone was just a soldier. Yet, he was a member of what would be called the greatest generation - *before there was even a war.* He wasn't quite war hero. He couldn't be. There was no war.

Not yet.

Not until during the pre-Christmas days of early December 1941 when word spread by radio and newspaper that a little-known harbor tucked inside the islands of Hawaii had been attacked by Japanese bomber planes, killing thousands of American soldiers, sailors and Marines. In short order Hitler's Axis Powers would join with the Empire of Japan and declare war on the United States. Men ran to enlist and join the military.

Tony Malone was already at the head of the line.

His wartime duties would take him to places that history books of today speak of in awe: fighting in North Africa, Sicily, D-Day, and ultimately to Hitler's Lair.

His helmet went with him — observing tales that even his family barely *if ever* knew.

Across the country in Grant's Pass, Oregon young 14-year-old Billy Mansfield heard the news of Pearl Harbor from his father, George. Too old to join, George Mansfield, in his late 30's knew he still had to defend his family in the event that the Japanese assault kept coming toward the west coast of California and Oregon. No stranger to shotguns and rifles, George had a reoccurring nightmare of Japanese soldiers para-chuting from the skies overhead onto his farm. In this night-terror, George found himself without his guns, holding only one thing in his hands — a pitchfork. Protecting his wife and two kids, George Mansfield, stood alone on the knoll of his farmland killing Impe-rial invaders as they fell from the skies in billowy and bloody parachutes.

While *George* was too old, *Billy* was too young. One had nightmares of war while the other had daydreams of glory. 1941 quickly became 1942 and then '43, '44 and finally '45. Soldiers kept joining the war effort. Millions of them. But not Bill Mansfield.

Many WWII soldiers were too young to actually serve in combat during WWII. Still they joined the service; and very quickly many bore the shame of military wannabes from the 40's — a pain that they tried to salve for the rest of their life by claiming WWII military status.

In a sense they *were* accurate — strange as it seems. Hundreds of thousands of men were sworn-in to the military prior to VJ Day, so their names *are* numbered with those whose ribbons quietly show actual WWII service. Yet, they themselves did nothing. They wanted to fight, however they were just too late. Men who missed the boat.

Like my dad, who at age 17, entered the US Navy in October 1945 but never sailed to war.

Bill Mansfield, feeling as if he was losing out and shameful in his own eyes of being too young, pushed the limits to become a member of the military at 17. He was finally accepted into the US Navy.

Hoping to see something in combat. *Anything.*

But he saw nothing.

Nothing like Sgt. Malone saw.

And even the teenage version of my dad knew it.

As Private Malone was grabbing his weapon in the US on Pearl Harbor Day, Bill Mansfield was grabbing a football as a junior high student. As A.J. Malone was being shipped out to the war zone, Bill Mansfield was a freshman in high school. The world was at war and Malone was answering the call. Bill Mansfield, however, was only seeing his uncles join the Navy and Marine Corps, not himself. The young soldier-wannabe waited for Father Time's moving the clock's hands, week after week, strange battlefield names — one after another.

And A.J. Malone fought in almost every one of the strangely named European and North African battles. He held soldiers as they died in his Medic arms. He then gently laid down each dead young man's body, taking a dog tag, only to follow the cries of the next wounded warrior of the battlefield, as they yelled with all that was in them: "Medic! Medic!"

While Sgt. A.J. Malone and his Band of Brothers made their way into the very mountain resort of Nazi Germany's Adolf Hitler, Seaman WE Mansfield simply read about it in the papers, back in The States.

He was too late to be a warrior in WWII.

That warrior thing would have to wait until Korea exploded a few years later. He would indeed be deployed into a war zone and serve with honor there. It was however a lesser war to many Americans, "a police action", a United Nations conflict. And many men who hoped for glory simply found gore, and death and boredom: nothing like they had read about in Time and Life magazines from the first half of the 1940's.

Bill would never be in combat. He would have to forgive himself for that fact. It was not for him to be a WWII combat veteran and he had to come to the point that it was alright to forgive himself for simply being too young.

He was too young to wear a WWII uniform or US Army helmet — either a doughboy one like A.J. Malone's or any other kind.

But years later, he would buy one.

And give it to his son.

Little did he know that a simple Christmas gift to his 15-year-old son would, *in return*, touch the lives of the original owner's wife, their daughters and all hero-soldier's grandkids as well as so many more people, helping them heal.

It also was a part of his own healing. That he would become a hero to a hero's family was healing indeed.

Searching for Malone helped Bill Mansfield search for himself.

He just didn't know it, yet.

The Christmas wrapping-paper hadn't yet been removed.

Chapter 5

A father's gift to his son

The year was 1971 and I was a 15-year-old high school sophomore who loved American history. In many ways I was not the right teen for that decade. I was somehow miscast.

America in the hot summer months of 1971 was embroiled in an unpopular war, anti-war fervor was rampant on many high school and college campuses. Angry white college kids vented their angst at TV cameras, university professors and their parents. Racial riots were tearing apart those same campuses and adjoining towns, caused by a deep dislike of the very history that I loved — or at least the very history that I thought I knew and therefore loved. Angry black kids, not able to be sent to college took an equal stake in tearing apart their own city blocks and those of the white families, whose children were off at college, protesting. It was a destructive and terrible circle of youthful rage, regardless of skin color.

Detroit Michigan and its suburbs were not the cutting edge of anti-war campus unrest, yet the racial tensions of 1971 did find welcome arms in old-area places like Detroit, Indianapolis, and other rusting northern cities; century-old cities where manufacturing once held sway, as the most productive of industries to have and to hold through the marriage of municipal growth and urban renewal. The parts of the cities that weren't falling down were being quickly and quietly torn down for a "brighter future". And in most cases that meant, tearing down the neighborhoods, which bore the title "slum" — often in the black communities. The feelings of unjust actions by men in power was debilitating to the young black and white men and women who felt they could accomplish *nothing* constructive, so they resorted to doing *everything* destructive.

Causing angry teens to take to the streets.

We lived on one of those streets in nearby Mt. Clemens, Michigan — and ours was apparently the dividing line between the "white" neighborhood and the "black" one. Our alley was our neighbors' alley. Different skin color, same school, different understandings of history, same trashcans. We were friends and neighbors.

When hotheaded young black rioters wanted to attack a convenient white neighborhood, our street seemed to surface to the top.

Except for a minor problem - our black neighbors came to our aid. African American dads who had served in the military stood on the porch with my father, himself a veteran. These men knew how to meet force with force. Their weapons cradled in their black and white arms told the rioters to move away.

And they did move away, quickly.

It soon became the autumn of 1971.

Joe Maguire sent me a small package along with a letter just a few months before Christmas. In the letter, dated September 11th, 1971 he wrote about the history of his father-in-law, my Great Grandfather. He reminded me that this man whom I had never met was elected to an office, served with distinction and when he passed away the very gavel with which he used to preside over meetings had been given to a very young Joe Maguire — who used it for over a half a century more.

Enclosed with that letter in the package was the gavel! He wanted an item of family heritage to become the property of a mere 15-year-old boy. Joe Maguire ended his letter with this simple well-turned and memorable phrase, "(T)his gavel, while verging on antiquity, is actually priceless". "Rule wisely with it", he directed me.

Grand Pop understood his heritage as well as understanding my future interest in politics. He gave to me what many kids of the 1960's never received from their fathers and grandfathers — a legacy. His extended visits, though infrequent, were cherished times of laughter, slight-of-hand illusion tricks and reading of books out loud to my siblings and me.

I held his gavel in my teenage hands and marveled at where it had been: Denver, Hartford, Boston, Washington DC, Baltimore and Harrisburg PA.

I've carried on the service of my Great Grandfather by using it into adulthood. I treasured that gift - then and now. His gavel rests with his letter on a shelf in my home office...until recently when I gave it to my son, who is a cadet at West Point. He uses it there.

I remember watching the news coverage on TV the year before of the horrible Kent State shootings and killings — a university that called in the National Guard to control the out-of-control college students. Young people were shot, some killed by equally young soldiers with government issued weapons and long-held beliefs in the America they served. I could relate to the young guardsmen. I could not relate to the anti-war college kids. I could however grieve with the parents of the young adults who protested and died.

I could not understand their anger at our nation's heritage — expressed by both the young white and young black kids.

Into this confusing convergence of hatred, disappointment and anger came the latest December edition of the annual blanketing by snow of the Michigan countryside. CS Lewis's famed quote of winter and Christmas in Narnia seemed only to partially apply during this uneasy wintry truce. The desperately cold soul of Detroit's winter only slightly acknowledged that it was Christmas, and that for but a few lone days.

And it was in that interval of Christmas that I received the single best gift my parents ever gave me.

The questioning looks from my siblings said much as I undid the gift-wrapping on Christmas morning. The box was clunky, wrapped well, but oddly shaped. I knew my dad was fastidious in his wrapping of presents, my mom, less so. In some ways the goofy size of the present combined with the well-tucked and tightly wrapped nativity scene images showed me that the wrapping of this gift was a joint parental project.

I was right.

The wrapping papers quickly fell to the side under my watch, the box beckoned for me to gently unfasten its lid, weigh the gift on my lap, guessing its weight at 10-12 pounds and then open it.

"A helmet!" I shouted. "You *actually* got me a helmet!! A doughboy helmet for Christmas, Dad? *Thank you so much.*" And I hugged my father with an unusual show of exuberance — knowing in my "knower" that my dad bought it for me, *probably* against my mom's wishes - and knowing that my mom was somewhere in the kitchen fixing the eggnog, shaking her head gently and laughing at how easy it was to placate her third-born male child.

I was ecstatic.

It was a WWI-era helmet, the kind you see in old movies or pre-Pearl Harbor documentaries on

America's ill-prepared soldiery prior to Hitler and the Axis Powers. British in style it seemed to be well worn and had the look and feel of a piece of history, unlike anything I had ever owned. At 15 years of age, I had owned very little that I could call history. But on *that* December 25th in 1971, I owned a helmet that had most likely seen things I had only read about in long-yellowed books on war.

Many decades later, when the wonders and mysteries of this story unfolded, my *then*-81 year-old father wrote about what had happened on that fateful day he bought the helmet.

He wrote: "I remember they held up this dirty old helmet and asked for $2.99… nobody bid on it…then for *one reason or another* I got to thinking about my son, Dennis …and that I could clean it up for him. I offered (the winning bid of) one dollar and seventy-five cents… and went home and cleaned up my treasure. While doing so, I noticed the name "Malone" hand-printed inside it."

The gift was given to me and I received it. I DO remember at the time seeing the inexpensive price-marking on the inside of the helmet and also briefly thinking, "Boy he sure got off easy with *my* Christmas gift." I also remember shaking off that flinching emotion and choosing to be happy that I owned a part of history, regardless of the price.

I kept the helmet on a shelf, over my study desk at my parents' home till I graduated from high school.

It stared down at me from its perch on the shelf, when I put on my first tux to take a lovely young girl to the prom; and it seemed to occupy a special space in my room for my younger brother and sisters, who loved to just come in and talk to me about life and history.

It peered from the shelf, next to my gavel, when I received a Presidential Appointment to West Point and it traveled with me to the United States Military Academy. It sat on another shelf, peering down.

A silent part of military history looked down from a shelf-perch at the premier of all military schools — West Point. Though this granite gray university taught about war, the helmet I held in my possession seemed to hold closer, unknowable mysteries that enveloped its olive drab color and brown leathery chinstrap.

I stored the helmet next to my gavel. I used the gavel when I presided as President of my class at the West Point. I used the helmet as a reminder to myself of those who went before me to fight for our nation.

Little did I realize that I held in my possession *both* symbols of what was taught at West Point: *law and order.*

Though the motto of the Military Academy is Duty, Honor, Country — the application of that motto is through law and order.

Later, I found out, that the owner of the helmet saw action in WWII, not WWI. It was a doughboy US Army Helmet that held eyewitness secrets of the bloody sands of North Africa, the gritty landing of D-Day, the frozen Battle of the Bulge and the ultimate triumphant entry into Adolf Hitler's Alpine Wolf's Lair.

Through military strength, these young soldiers of the 40's brought law and order to a world ripped apart by lawless tyrants.

Little did I know, that unlike the priceless gavel received from my beloved grandfather, there was a family somewhere out there that was missing a piece of their heritage, a helmet with a name inside it, which I now owned.

Both were gifts given within weeks of each other.

Where the gavel was a clearly connected symbol of justice and love that had a crystal clear chain of title to its ownership, the helmet was for all intents and purposes, anonymous.

The gavel was a priceless gift, given by a grandfather who loved me.

The helmet was a cheap present given by a father who did not.

I could never have been more wrong.

Chapter 6

Gifts as a part of the Languages of Love

Forgiveness always triumphs over abuse, disrespect and pain. It is a part of the languages of God's love.

And each of us understands that language in different ways.

In Gary Chapman's classic breakthrough work, The 5 Love Languages, he makes a very accurate compilation of the essential languages of love we all use.

They are:

Acts of service
Words of affirmation
Physical touch
Quality time
Gifts

Bill Mansfield's love language was expressed in the giving and receiving of gifts. For most of his life none of his children ever knew how to tell him that they loved him. Yet, if we would have paid attention, it was through the giving of gifts to him.

The signs of that as his love language were many and frequent. He simply wanted to say to others, "I love you," and did so by giving gifts. Few were listening.

Every business trip that my dad went on created an exciting time when he returned. He'd always have small gifts and tokens of appreciation tucked away in his suitcase, things that he'd bring to my siblings and me.

They ranged from small toys to the proverbial packets of peanuts, that he could easily have thrown away. After New Years parties, he always made an effort to bring home those funny and colorful celebration hats that adults used to wear in the 50's and 60's while they watched Guy Lombardo's band bring in the New year. Martinis, cigarettes and funny hats were the order of the evening for the adults.

The funny hats, were his gifts to us the next morning when we arose.

Christmas mornings were always awash with an array of presents that covered the floor; it was hard to find a patch of carpet, amid the hundreds of wrapped packages.

When I was 17 years old, my Dad asked me if I would like to take a look at cars for sale. Like any junior in high school, I was always looking at cars for sale! Knowing that my dad was well-versed on automobiles, as well as the crafty ways that salesmen sold them, I more than needed his help. So we lit out to see what was there.

Southern California has several beautiful long, narrow yet somehow spacious valleys that make up the southland. Along the 10 Freeway, the San Gabriel Valley is home to several lovely bedroom communities, each sharing long rambling roads that run perpendicular to the massive thoroughfare. Among these communities are the cities of Covina and West Covina.

Covina was founded first. It's south of Glendora, east of Azusa and west of Pomona. Boulevards with the names Citrus Avenue, Barranca, Lark Ellen cross north through the many winding city boundaries.

But there's a problem. These two Covinas are liars to each other. Or at least the city fathers were directionally challenged. West Covina is actually south of Covina. As a young driver, I never quite saw where one city boundary ended and another began and I sure as heck never got north-south directions. It was a jumbled mess of nonsense to the teenage version of me.

On the night of our car-trolling, my dad and I traveled up Citrus Avenue, casually seeking for-sale-by-owner signs. We were on a sort–of dad and son mini road trip, looking for wheels. West Covina ended somewhere along the way. Covina appeared all at once, equally mysteriously.

We were just driving, not stopping and not particularly spotting anything worthy of even slowing down to see.

Suddenly Dad pulled into a little car dealership on Citrus Avenue specializing in Volvos.

Volvos? Seriously?

Those boxy foreign-looking cars for the snow? I remember thinking, "What in the world are we doing here? He is NOT going to find me some Swedish family station wagon, is he?"

It was apparent that I didn't know my dad.

We pulled in and got out of his car. As we meandered about the small lot, he casually pointed to a low-lying forest green '67 Austin Healy Sprite convertible resting comfortably in the midst of a parking lot full of family cars. It looked like the kissin' cousin of an MG Midget.

I turned to him with a furrowed face of confusion. He smiled.

I will never forget what he did next. Bill Mansfield reached into his pocket, pulled out a set of keys he obviously already owned and then, as my memory, cluttered by even 40 years of many other wonderful moments, recalls how in what seemed like slow motion, he swung his right arm and hand in almost a softball pitch way towards me, tossing the keys through the air. His voice, *captured for the rest of my life*, said four simple words. "It's yours, son, enjoy!"

Like so many of us, Dad's language was not everyone else's language.

And if he didn't understand another person's love language, he simply wrote them off as "s.o.b's". Very little compassion escaped over the wall once the language barrier was constructed.

And very little compassion was extended *to him*, as well.

People either loved him or hated him.

It just so happened that in time many in his work environment loved him and no one at home shared that same feeling—at least not in his first marriage, the one that involved my mother.

Christmases were chock full of presents that covered the whole carpet, the entire entry floorboards and well under the tree. Santa's photo was snapped on numerous occasions, stockings had more candy in them than we were EVER allowed to eat as kids—thus fully substantiating the reality that our parents were NOT Santa Claus.

And the Christmas of '71 brought the only gift, other than through memories, which would remain with me for almost four decades.

By giving a single gift of a helmet, Bill Mansfield set into motion a series of amazing and unplanned-for events, covering a period of 41 years that would eventually heal the relationship with his son, change his own life and usher him into eternity as a man changed by the love of God.

In attempting to find A. J. Malone, my dad and I clearly captured incremental, nuanced movement toward the Father God who loved us both. He became the father that both of us needed.

It happened in little bits and pieces, through heartache and being broken. Like soldiers taking a steep and costly hill or mountain, one meter at a time, we came as soldiers climbing a mount called Calvary. We were both honored once we got there.

Receiving honor is a strange thing. We can't successfully demand it of ourselves. Only others can extend it to us and only we can give it to others. Once received, it rests securely in the hands of the one honored, and will not be dislodged by lies or falsehoods.

Extending forgiveness is like that, too. It can't be demanded of us to forgive someone. We must choose to forgive another person and once forgiven, no one else can take that away from the two parties involved.

Hope, however, can be taken away by others. It can be crushed either intentionally or accidentally under the heel of insensitive people. Once deferred, our hearts ache from hope's absence.

There exists a strange three-way semi-elastic tension between hope, honor and forgiveness. All of us are firmly dependent on at least two of these words working together at key intersections of our lives: Honor and forgiveness. Hope, however has a tendency to come and go.

When hope noticeably fades, honor and forgiveness become choices of will; the actions that flow from those choices can change one's life and, if allowed to spread, can change the world.

We honor people when we ask for, as well as accept, forgiveness.

Then, oddly enough... hope returns to a much wider audience. People are watching. More people than we can fully know are impacted.

Honor, forgiveness and hope are free to move together once more.

How these three things impact the five languages of love and how the result takes various shapes, over long periods of time, ultimately can come at us when we least expect it.

Occasionally a story remains with us because it endures the ravages of time, protected by a strange and beautiful series of providential events, encasing and protecting the moments of our lives, gently inviting those moments as guests into the available space of our lives today.

If we let it, a story like that can invite us also into the

lives, and days, of loved ones. If allowed the opportunity, it introduces adult sons and daughters to unknown versions of their once-youthful parents. In many ways, we can never know our mothers and fathers by simply living with them. Not really. It often takes distance and perspective.

And time.

How fitting that the endurance and protection of such a story can be tied to time; as well as by objects given to us by strangers.

More often than not, it's family that gives us gifts.

Turned calendar pages allow children to eventually become adult children, while parents can grow older, obtaining grace and silver haired strands of wisdom, if they choose to.

One object might be a long-since-forgotten love letter, penned decades ago by a bride to her then-new soldier/husband; the passions of a tender couple burning brightly on its pages.

Another, a simple friendly letter of hope *and* future, accidentally stuffed into the recesses of a trunk or dresser drawer, abandoned long after the recipient of the letter had lived, returned home, loved and died. Often, browned photos, once black and white, silently bear witness that a man in uniform once lived — a man whose last name you or I may even bear.

I stumbled on just such a letter while researching the book you have in your hands. It was written to me by my father while I was in my very painful freshman year at West Point. I had not seen or read it in almost 40 years. Key excerpts are as follows:

Monday, April 14, 1975
Dear W. Dennis,

Received your letter of the 8th and must say I was very moved by the sincerity of your words. Thank you very much. It's kindness such as this that makes being a parent a worthwhile project of life. There is one thing that the good Lord does not provide us with and that's a roadmap as to the best possible way to grow up and raise our offspring...

I know that I can do anything that I set my cap to do... maybe not as good as some do it, but by darn it gets done. Not brag, just fact. That's the reason that you had a hard time with me... I only want you to avoid the pitfalls that are hidden in life.

(Y)ou (three older kids) are all on your own to do with yourselves as you see fit. God bless you for being part of my life. I must now concentrate on what's left (I'll most likely be a much different father to the remaining portion of four kids) and with your help they will grow up to know what it means to stick with something and make it conform to what you think it ought to be...

I fear that you have had a false notion that I loved the service... I wonder at times that this idea and then dispose of it as being caused by the fact that I spent so long a time in the military... I hated it at times (more times than I loved it and that's for sure). I hated the unnecessary waste of talent such as putting a technician on KP (kitchen patrol), wool uniforms (you haven't lived till you wear a heavy wool uniform in the heat of summer. Yes, my boy I hated it on many occasions. I got into trouble once in awhile because of my convictions...but knew when to pull in my horns before my children would have to visit me behind a fence... haha... I loved the appropriate uniform, the flag, the spit and polish, the parades and the music, the admiration of my men... the very fact they believed in my capabilities, honesty, forthrightness and morality. I do not think that I ever intentionally let one of my men (or officers) down.

I wanted to be an officer. I had my chance at OCS (Officer Candidate School), passed the entrance exams and then met an obstacle...Mom didn't want to be left alone for six-months.

I know how tough it is to be a plebe son. The secret is to pull in your horns BEFORE they get lopped off!

Close for now... and BREAK A LEG.
Lovingly, Dad

He said more in this letter than what was on the written page. Even today I feel the awkward attempt at love and the painful pang of his brokenness and self-absorption, even as I re-read it. He tried to do the best he could with what he had.

That such a written note of care, of attempted intimacy and concern from a father to his son away at school could be set aside, the discovery of it being left somewhat to happenstance and the possible peering eyes of future (and unknown) progeny, is enough for some family members to demand, upon their own demise, the burning of any such letters. In my dad's case, he showed so much about himself in such a vulnerable fashion. He never let down his men, but regularly let down his kids and they were crushed.

There are times when sons and daughters, raised under the roofs of hard parents occasionally enjoy the pleasure of seeing their parents in love.

When a letter IS discovered, the next generation gets to discover a cache of inked heartbeats, which at one time stirred up a natural expression of joy and intimacy between their parents. When that happens there is no accidental blushing of those two or three generations. All parties benefit from it.

Yet, as in my family's case, there are *no* letters of love between parents which unite lovers, sons and grand-sons — instead, the uniting is accomplished through an unanticipated gift. When we're fortunate, the center of a tale can be found in a very simple object — an old car, a clapboard house, a wooden box in a grandparent's dusty attic — protecting a note of a previous generation from the ravages of current war.

Sometimes it even takes strangers.

How much more fitting to this story that the object of this *protection* turned out to be a soldier's rusted, yet well-worn helmet. The hand-scribbled inscription inside the helmet simply read: *"A.J. Malone, Co 'H' 16th med. Reg't, Ford Devens, Mass."*

That stranger.

Someone neither my dad nor I knew, but we wanted to.

PAYING TRIBUTE
to
A STANGER

Bill Mansfield's Military honors
and medals 1945-1966

Bill Mansfield's 9 kids:
Front Row: Cheri, Joyce, Kathy, and Janet.
Back: JoAnne, Dennis, Ken, Gary, and Diane.

CMSGT (Ret) William Mansfield
and his wife Marilyn. "We've had a
good life, haven't we?"

Marilyn and Bill and their grand-
daughter Christy Burich.

The Legacy of Bill and Marilyn Mansfield: grandkids and great-grand-
daughter.

Almost a year after Dad died. Continuing the family way of enjoying life.

The romance of WWII. Love began when the war ended. Marine Corps Sgt. Virginia "Ginny" Maguire and Seaman 1st Class Bill Mansfield.

Sgt. Ginny Maguire during WWII. Fetching and tender, forceful and kind. She was always faithful.

The joy of seeing WWII come to an end. Seaman 1st Class Bill Mansfield and his ability to perform.

Changing uniforms; after WWII the Navy loses to Army. Bill Mansfield joins the Army Air Corps.

August 1947, Bill and
Ginny Mansfield on a very
happy wedding day.

In Korea and alone; Bill Mansfield's wished for war experiences
would not be in Europe or the
Pacific.

Staff Sgt. Bill Mansfield in Tagu Korea.
Too young for WWII, he served well
during the Korean War.

Bill and Ginny. Living the life
in the 1950's.

My Grand Pop and me, 1960's. He taught me that humor and seriousness could easily abide together.

Mr. & Mrs. John J. Maguire, 1960's. Grand Pop was a larger than life figure for a boy to easily follow.

My family that profited from me honoring my dad; Caleb, Cole and Meg Roe, my bride, Susan and my son, Colin at my daughters college graduation, 2012.

Christmas Morning, 1971 and a fifteen year old. AJ Malone's helmet became Dennis Mansfields most notable gift.

My father's many stripes, but not enough-He almost became the first Chief Master Sergeant of The Air Force.

Susan and Colin; West Point Mama and her Cadet son at The Army Navy Game, 2012, Philadelphia-the city that started it all.

The last photo of my Dad and me. I looked into his eyes and haltingly told him I would never see him again. He knew.

MSGT William Mansfield and his grandson, West Point Cadet Colin Mansfield together salute the flag.

Two soldiers honoring one another.

The US Air Force Honor Guard at CMSGT William E. Mansfield's funeral, 2012.

Bill Mansfield, 1927-2012. Son, husband father, grandfather. His last words wer "We've had a good life. Haven't we?"

Sgt. Anthony J. Malone, WWII Veteran. The hero who wore the helmet.

The students from Vineyard Boise at the grave of AJ Malone.

The widow of AJ Malone, Mary being interviewed after accepting the helmet back from the students.

Chapter 7

Education, Students and a Helmet

Pink Floyd's classic song and music video, *Another Brick in the Wall,* opens with these lyrics:

We don't need no education.
We don't need no thought control.
No dark sarcasm in the classroom.
Teacher, leave those kids alone.
All in all it's just another brick in the wall.

The lyrics of the song and the images of the music video seem to illustrate something very profound.

No child learns when forced to do so.

And we are blessed as a nation to have teachers who are changing methods of educating kids. Education in America has in the past been tailored to forcing its vast amount of students into auditory, sequential learners. Whether they fit or not.

These are students who learn by listening, while proceeding through a chronological curriculum sequence. If a student learns well through listening, then it's a terrific outcome. If not? The images on the Pink Floyd video come to mind. It's not the intention of the teachers to do so, it's the historical system that makes it so.

Very few things that we, as a nation, did a century ago would make the cut as methods we should still employ today. Transportation, printing, energy, athletics, politics, etc all are done differently now. Most of the methods of the late nineteenth and early twentieth centuries have yellowed with age and were discarded.

But somehow, teaching as it was done a century ago still survives today in many quarters, almost completely intact.

And the picture of the classroom remains much the same as well. It doesn't matter whether it's public or private education.

All in all it's just another brick in the wall. And many hard working teachers are purposely choosing to knock down that wall. It's exciting to observe.

Many American high school classes are still replete with 30+ desks, occupied by 30+ different students, rotating each hour into and out of those seats and desks. Class subjects change. English grammar gives way to foreign language verbs being conjugated. Math tests cover the desks in another class hour. Regardless of the subject being covered, the four walls of the room remain the same as students move in and out, and inquisitive, overachievers still sit near the front needing to be close to the teacher/professor just as they did 100 years ago. The underachievers sit near the back, closer to the door for the potentially imminent pardon and reprieve brought about by an anonymous finger pushing an irritating buzzer, creating an even more irritating bell to ring.

Learning takes place regardless for those who learn through traditional auditory means.

For example, what of the visual learner and the kinesthetic learner? The ones who have either a need to view and/or touch the material being studied? Those methods are being tackled with great success.

Freedom has many costs: in formal public and private education settings the cost is time. In fact, for those students who dislike learning, education can often look like incarceration. For the disinterested American student, waiting for the bell to ring takes an entire class period of anticipation. These disinterested students, bored to tears learn patience, if nothing else, through the tick-tick-tick taskmaster of time.

They tend to be given lip service by many old-style educational professionals, only to find out that *lips* need *ears* (auditory learners) to hear and therefore understand. It's a pathetic cycle in which many students simply do not learn, or better yet, they learn to pretend to learn, so that they can pass tests and gain an unreflective grade in a subject that means nothing to them. In many cases, these classes only serve as cocktail conversation in later years when, as professionals in their late twenties, as the classmates tell horribly blunt stories of failed high school teachers who stood in the front of classrooms only to have no one hear them.

It has been a system of one-size fits all for a long time and it does not fit well. Unless the educator has a different take on learning. Many educators are choosing new directions.

It was into a creative and amazingly different setting that I was asked to teach 11th grade history and choose a different take on learning.

I said "yes".

The key factor was that these 11th grade students met only twice a week in the classroom. They were home-schooled students.

In the creative world of alternative education, home-schooled students have a nice and pleasant reputation when they are elementary aged kids. Even home-schoolers in middle school or junior high seem to enjoy an acceptance by adults as well-bred young-adults. *Mini-adults.* And the mothers and fathers glow from such comments about their student-offspring.

It's at that point that high school presents itself.

If they don't watch it, like beautiful little child-actor stars in feature films, home-schooled kids tend to grow a type of awkwardness about themselves. No, not about social interaction — for these students have indeed mastered the ability to talk with adults on any subject; they tend to sound like adults when they speak up on this issue or that social concern.

No, the awkwardness is actually just regular teenage awkwardness: the gangly, all-arms-and-legs look - the bad skin and goofy hair look. The child star is no longer cute.

The *mini-adult* is no longer mini.

When strict religious views are added to the mix, home schooling can start to resemble a type of Amish non-paradise — a place where long skirts and dull curriculum combine with brothers named Jedediah who love to read magazines on rocketry.

In many ways, these students in my history class were the most non-home-schooled kids I had ever seen. My wife and I had been greatly influenced by Dr. Raymond Moore, the dean of home-schooling, in the late twentieth century. We listened to Dr. Moore's radio interviews with internationally respected child psychologist, Dr. James Dobson and decided to give it a try. That try lasted twenty-two-years and three children... *none of whom were named Jedediah, by the way.*

At The Vineyard Christian Home School Co-op (VCHSC) in our home town of Boise, Idaho, the students spend two days in a classroom setting and then three days per week motivated to learn at their own pace and through their own style of learning, at their own home.

It was home-schooling without the weirdo feel.

Several of the high school juniors in my class were already choosing college courses and trips abroad. One was planning to spend his college time in Australia, another at the United States Military Academy at West Point, still others were planning on working their way through local colleges and universities by getting jobs. They were serious kids with an infectious sense of humor. Many had experienced loss. One young lady successfully warded off a brain tumor, which unfortunately left its mark by robbing her of her ambulatory ability. She could think, talk and love people; she simply could not walk well.

These responsible young men and women were the ones into whose hands a most unusual research project fell.

And it happened in a most unexpected way.

The original history teacher suddenly resigned just days before school started in September. When I was called upon to suddenly take over VCHSC's history class, I chose to do two things. First, I accepted the position to help the school's principal, who was rightfully beside herself with concern. It seemed easy in one respect — my son was in the class, I knew many of the other students and I was self employed — allowing me the freedom to set aside a mere two one-hour blocks per week to help. Helping out is what parents are supposed to do with their kids' education, right?

Yes, especially since it's not a lot of time. Simple math. No problem. My help would be *easy* to extend.

The second reason I accepted the yearlong position was that they agreed to my proposal that I could teach history backwards.

My childhood love of history bent me in this direction. As a young student I often asked *why* an event had happened.

For example, as a ten-year-old child while living with my family in San Antonio, Texas I visited the famed Alamo with my fourth grade class. The scene of Texas' virtual cradle of independence was fully entombed as both a sacred battlefield and holy birthplace for every man's freedom. I was captivated by the many lives of the men who came, fought and died at the Mission San Antonio de Alamo. Yet, the nagging question was simple in my mind: where were these men before they arrived on the banks of the Noche del Rio? How did men from Tennessee arrive together as a fighting force? How did the former US Congressman David Crockett gain the leadership of that group and how did he receive his colonelcy? My fourth-grade mind raced backwards to find the reasons.

Fill in the blank as the years continued on, I always wondered, "What occurred to make that happen?"

Historical issue by historical issue, event by event — it was my way to think backwards through history.

So, if VCHSC needed a history teacher and I was being asked to fill that empty slot, then my up-front contract would be to teach history backwards.

The principal agreed to my rather unorthodox plan.

We also reached an agreement that the class would be *pass/fail*. Being the husband of a school teacher who spent copious amounts of time grading papers, while filling in little tiny grades into even smaller and less legible grade spaces, I had no time nor interest to do so myself.

Two days a week? Roger.

Backwards history" Check.

Pass/fail? Yep.

Okay, I'm in.

What I didn't realize was what I was in *for...*

Within days, the next words I heard were these: "The good news, Mr. Mansfield, is you're hired, the bad news is you're promoted..."

Say what?

Was this a joke? Good news/bad news jokes always

leave me wondering what types of people actually link those two thoughts together. The mere thought of anything being bad news bodes ill for either the giver or the receiver, it *always* seems.

When the issues are in fact *not* a joke, the complete complexity of the situation presents itself.

That's what happened to me.

VCHSC is a very unique education environment. Begun in Lancaster, California over 25 years ago, the school along with its founder, Tri Robinson and his wife Nancy, migrated north to Idaho shortly after it started. It happened when a pioneering band of hearty souls, led by the educator-turned-pastor left the high desert of California and moved to Idaho to establish the Boise Vineyard, bringing VCHSC with them.

The first group of home school parents and children planned out the method by which the school would operate: traditional classroom teaching would occur on Tuesdays and Thursdays and home schooling would happen the other days of the week. Parents could, if chosen, become teachers for the co-op. All students were challenged to become self-directed scholars, no matter what their grade.

They do it the same way today.

And the idea caught on in Idaho. The school grew, new classes were added, new teachers hired, new subjects studied.

For many years, the school was K-6. In time, though, 7th and 8th grades were added and with one final push, a high school was born in the autumn of 2006, ultimately graduating its first Senior High School Class in 2010.

And it was with *that* class, in their *junior* year, that I walked to the front of the classroom one fresh autumn morning in 2008 and picked up a marker to write my name on the white board.

"I am your teacher, my name is Mr. Mansfield." Many of the kids snickered in a fun way. They knew me as "Colin's dad". A couple close friends knew me as *Dennis*.

Near the end of the first day, I was asked to come meet with the then-senior pastor. A keen educator, son of an educator, Tri Robinson breathes educational curriculum in and out. His father finished his own educational career at Beverly Hills High School as principal, corralling some of Hollywood's famed celebrity children and child stars. Tri's educational arena was less glitzy, resembling more the hard ridden cowboy leather of Palmdale and Lancaster's public schools. Tri took that rode-hard-and-put-away-wet attitude into his blossoming Boise church as well as the transplanted hybrid home school he founded. In time the church would have a membership of over 2,500 and the school boast an attendance of 200 students, plus a teaching staff of 22.

And the educator-turned-pastor wanted to talk to the

businessman-turned-first-day-teacher. *Why?*

Part of me wondered if someone with a much better academic vitae, employing a fuller, more realistic perspective regarding who should be teachers had gotten to him. The natural result being that I was "found out" and would be asked to leave.

"Um, Dennis, we realized we made a huge mistake…" was what I near-expected to greet me as I entered his office. He and the then-Executive Pastor of the church, Trevor Estes, looked quite grave, which only intensified and sharpened my leap-frogging of the embarrassing moment, by clearing my throat and beginning to mouth the words, "I understand".

But the message they delivered was not what I expected.

"Our principal unexpectedly resigned today. We have no one on staff who has management experience as you do. Will you take her position?" Tri said.

Short, sweet and to the point.

Hired one day, to be a teacher, promoted the next day to principal.

I had to chuckle. My wife, Susan, had served as a teacher at this lovely, innovative school for 6 years. She also received her California lifetime teaching certificate as a public school teacher in the late 1970's. Many of her then-students were now in their late-30's.

She home schooled our three children with very little input by me.

And here I was being asked to become her boss!

My chuckle moved to a full-fledged laugh.

I told the two pastors that I would need a day to think about it. I received a 24-hour period to think it over and went in search of a 9th grade teacher named Mrs. Mansfield.

I shared the news to her and we both sat pensively thinking about the ramifications. We went to dinner to talk about it some more. I *already had* a job.

You see, many years before, my wife and I, along with others, started a major business to counsel and educate ex-addicts who were *also* ex-inmates, as they transitioned from incarceration to freedom. I had a staff of many professionals and we had the investment dollars of other fine folks enmeshed in this going business concern. The responsibilities had been very heavy. The time commitments were brutal. I still had a high school aged son at home. In short order, I began transitioning myself out of the chief executive officer role. My business partner was more than able to fill my shoes in running the company, especially the real estate portion of the company. We brought aboard a gifted business consultant to handle the rest of the duties.

The goal of the firm was for men and women wishing to disengage from the drug culture, to make their abode with us in one of our 19 homes — working toward full sobriety in Christ-centered curriculum. My business partner, Mac, and I knew how important such a staffed, safe and sober environment is. We both had adult sons who were addicts.

Since I had another son who was a junior in high school… and his school needed a principal it seemed the right timing for me to help. I had time in my schedule to help.

The decision was actually quite easy to make. I realized I could be a part of helping these students become lifetime learners.

At the end of the 24 hours, I met with the two pastors and said *yes* to their proposal. The journey of a thousand historical stories was about to begin for me as teacher *and* principal, a novice at both.

Little did I know that my ignorance of what principals could and could not do was exactly what was needed to open the doors of a series of life-changing events — reaching from the wooded river city of Boise to the halls of the US Congress and then to the many snow covered small towns of Connecticut.

My single day of teaching had not quite prepared me to become the school's principal; at least not in a conventional career pathway.

No, instead I was an explorer, reorganizing the paper trail of history, in a backwards way to a group of extremely smart students. And I was the boss.

There was no good news/bad news joke here.

There was only the good news - helping students to look forward to see a world in their rear-view mirror.

Yes, I was all in.

I was all in and yet I *still* had no idea what that really meant.

Chapter 8
Finding A.J. Malone

Few would have thought that an accidental princi-pal-ship at a local Christian school would have set into motion the following: many hours of research by high school teens and their parents, as well as the involvement of a United States Congressman, the return to shared memories of the author and his father and the healing of the father about the effects of his own time in the US military. But that's what happened.

I was already a very busy businessman when I was asked to help the high school. An additional part of these new duties was to teach that history class of high school juniors. During the section of history that covers the two world wars, an ingenious idea hit me.

Why not challenge the juniors in high school to find the original owner of the helmet (or his heirs) and return it to them?

It seemed like a simple enough idea at the time.

The first phone call that went out was to my dad, asking everything that he knew about the helmet, its origins and what might be the best avenue of approach through which to return it.

To my surprise, in an instant, he reached back in his memory and said: "You mean return it to A.J. Maloney, er Malone? Wasn't that his name?"

I told him it was!

It seems the impression of the helmet had not been too far from my dad's memory. He told me he'd *always* wondered what had happened to the soldier who wore that one very special helmet.

Malone was the soldier who went to war and possibly died when Bill Mansfield lived, he seemed to quietly suggest.

Throughout history this was the shame of many returning soldiers who had survived war. Somehow, it seemed, finding Malone's family would be healing to my dad. In this particular moment, Dad and I began working together to see how this fledgling group of junior snoops and researchers could use their quite advanced skills on the Internet to hunt down the whereabouts of A.J. Malone, his family or his long lost heirs.

My dad was a pioneer in computers starting with his military service in 1945. His retirement from the military in the mid-sixties landed him right in the center of a budding civilian computer industry. He was always on the cutting edge of the next expansion all the way into the birthing of the Internet. When it came to using the internet to track down A.J. Malone, my dad was chock full of suggestions for me via email and phone. He loved this idea!

The students added their knowledge and skills. My teaching and research changed from a regular classroom setting to the school's computer lab. The class members began to feel at home in the lab.

The juniors worked hard in school and at home. As high school home educated students they were quite use to doing research from their kitchen tables.

Here's how they described it in their blog:

"As the student exploration began, we had only fragments of history in front of us. An old WWI helmet, a man's name, a Fort long forgotten. And 12 students who knew how to successfully surf the Internet and blog about it.

When (our history teacher) brought the helmet into our class, (we) thought it would simply be a kind of 'show and tell.'

It was...because this helmet went on to show (us) much.

It was ludicrous, insane, and impossible! The thought of our class being challenged to find the man whose name was written inside the helmet was simply unfeasible. A needle in a haystack....

How on earth could we hope to find this "A.J. Malone"? But, partly because of curiosity, and partly because our grades depended on it, the 11th grade class embarked on this journey. We spent about …four weeks researching."

They were four very long weeks. Intense research that started unfruitfully with serviceman records from WWI.

No matter what source the students pursued, there was no US Army member from WWI named A. J. Malone.

This created a perplexing development.

Was he a civilian doctor—connected somehow to the Medical detachment? Was he a British service member who came over to instruct others in America during WWI?

Every place we turned for WWI names and contacts ended in cul-de-sacs.

Then, one of the students suggested that the class pursue a different path—to sort of *back into* the search for Mr. Malone. I didn't quite grasp what the student was suggesting until this was said, "Forget about the soldier for a second and let's research the helmet, itself. Maybe that will shed light on something."

One of the high tech juniors focused deeply on the small things of the helmet and in a very short period of time became a bit of an expert on doughboy helmets. He knew the companies, he knew where they'd been manufactured and stored both during and after the war: Boston, NYC, Philadelphia and more.

After the war…. His mind started racing.

He came to the class and proposed a different scenario. What if A.J. Malone never served in WWI, but instead was a soldier in WWII?

We all quizzically looked at each other. "It's a WWI helmet, not a WWII helmet", one of the students spouted.

The helmet-expert ignored the obvious.

What if there existed a time period whether *prior to* or maybe *at the start of* WWII where the soldiers wore leftover uniforms from WWI?

We were dumbfounded.

WWII? The students went into a flurry of activity. Websites were turned upside down, lists were searched and PDFs of conscription records were downloaded and printed. The class searched WWII records from all over Massachusetts, again coming up empty handed, time and time again. They were forced to expand their circle of search to other New England states.

The students' blog picks up again from there.

"Mary Zimmerman was the first to finally make a breakthrough: she found A.J.'s army record through Google! Using the information found there as a springboard, we were able to delve further into Anthony's (that is his name) past; find out about the man, the mission, and the mandate.

And so our research took off! Opportunities began to open up, and things happened right before our eyes!

At about this time the press began doing pieces on our project: first the Idaho Statesman then Idaho News Channel 7 NBC affiliate KTVB. Suddenly our small semester helmet project was known by... people around our state (and nationwide through Associated Press)."

Like any painstaking research project, the mechanics were pedantic, restrained and took time - weeks and weeks of time. I suggested they tackle this website or that Veterans department. I was interested and wanted success for the students. The pace quickened.

From here, things were like a whirlwind.

A whirlwind, indeed. The students worked diligently to find out who A.J. Malone was, where he lived, who his family members were — whether he was alive or had passed away.

They were creating a tribute to him by their actions, not unlike what I did for my father on paper.

I found that I loved teaching these high school juniors and they loved learning. Lifetime learning has always been a part of my life — and I had the honor of sharing that love with these students.

Slowly but surely, the details about the helmet and its original owner were discovered by these young men and women. They found that Anthony J. Malone had passed away eight years before and that he was buried in Middletown, CT, where he had raised a family. Documents showed up. Obituaries were found. The paper trail became clear and concise.

The class found out that "Tony" Malone had military records and that his unit served in Sicily, mainland Italy and France. He had landed on D-Day and had climbed the Austrian mountains to Hitler's lair. Later we would find out that among his mementos he had a Nazi flag that he had taken off of Adolf Hitler's bedroom wall. As both a medic and an amateur photographer, he had been everywhere, helped many soldiers and recorded most of it in photographs.

During this time, Sgt. Malone also received a Purple Heart.

With all the facts assembled, the class was ready to announce their findings.

They had found Malone.

Now they needed to let his family know that they'd been searching for him! They found his family's addresses and phone numbers. The phone call went out to his family.

His widow, Mary Malone, still lived in the family home and had two adult daughters each of whom had families. Both sisters were cautious when the students called them to let them know of the research project.

One daughter later told me, "When they called, I honestly thought it was an Internet scam!"

I had to laugh. It was certainly about the Internet, but it was no scam!

Having established a connection with the Malone family, though vital to the project, they needed more. For the high school students to actually see their efforts bear fruit, they wanted to either bring a family member out to Idaho OR all of the students take the helmet back to Middletown, Connecticut to Mrs. Malone.

Word came to us quickly that Mary Malone was too frail to travel. If we wanted, they told us, the class could mail the helmet to the Malone family.

Fifteen motivated high school students would not let it stop there. "Nope," Shalom Knight said to her classmates, "we're going there!" The juniors began brainstorming ways that they could, as a class, fly out to Connecticut and personally return the helmet to Mrs. Malone and her entire family.

Word went out. These students contacted friends,

family, businesses and known travelers. They needed frequent flier miles — enough for them to travel. They'd need cash for lunches and dinners, so my son, Colin, asked his boss at the coffee shop drive through where he worked if he could take the helmet with him and have customers put money in the helmet as tips — to help them once they got to CT. Local print and radio media were called, the day was selected and coffee lovers came from everywhere. A business-woman invited Colin to come to their family business that same day and make a pitch to the employees. He got off work, went straight there, delivering a vivid description of all that they had done to reunite the helmet with the Malone family. The employees of Employer Resource responded. Colin walked away with the full and final amount the class needed for food and supplies. December's holiday sentiment provided a practical application of bringing gifts to these children. A.J. Malone's helmet was full of cash!

The only thing needed now was travel. Time was moving but we were not.

Soon it became the first weekend of January, 2009. The United States Congress had just been sworn in. Idaho's newest freshman US Representative, Walt Minnick. He had returned home to the Gem State andasked me if he could attend church with my family and me that Sunday. A gracious man, Walt wanted to reach out to his new constituents from his very first weekend as a US Congressman.

After church a student, Shalom Knight, came up to

me as I was saying goodbye to Congressman Minnick. She had no idea who he was. "Mr. Mansfield, I believe God is going to give us enough frequent flier miles for the whole class to go." She was a confident, secure young woman; simply stating a fact, in her mind. She was prayerful and powerful young 16-year-old. I mumbled something embarrassed and awkward at her bold statement of faith around this elected official. I quickly and dismissively thanked her and turned back to Walt.

"What does she mean, you need frequent flier miles? For what?" he asked.

I paused.

Then, I briefly told him the story of attempting to return the helmet to Sgt. Malone's widow and family and where we were in the process.

He looked at me and said, "I have 300,000 miles with US Airways and United and I'd like to give all of them to your students."

I was dumbstruck. I *really* couldn't speak.

"What… what?" was all I could mumble.

He stated, "I've got these miles from all my travels as a business man and a candidate, so why don't I just give them to your students? That's exactly what I'll do. You can use them a lot more than I could. And what better cause?"

That was that. Apparently, we were going.

As we worked with Congressman Minnick's staff to apply his frequent flier account number for the many tickets, we hit a snag. A big one.

Like other airlines, there are specific conditions for the use of mileage plus programs. For whatever reason, the system would not allow so many frequent flier miles to be used all at the same time for so many different people. The system simply said "no.

That is, until an angel in a US Airways uniform came to our rescue. Her name is Carole Cloyd and she was the Executive Services Manager for the DCA Club at Reagan International Airport in Washington D. C.

Carole saw what we were doing, coordinated the total logistics with her own company and United Airlines; she did exactly what it took to move a classroom of high school juniors from Boise, Idaho to Hartford, Connecticut and to do so via the help of a then-freshman Congressman Minnick. Carole brought joy and professionalism to this project that was infectious to the students and the parents! The Chief of staff for Walt Minnick, Mr. John Foster was outstanding in bringing all the pieces together.

Later, when the trip was completed, speaking for all the students, my son, Colin Mansfield, posted this on the class' blog:

"I am blown away by all the opportunities, experiences,

and miracles that have taken place. I am positive that God's hand has been on this trip from the very beginning.

The legacy of A.J. Malone is an incredible one, and I feel so honored and blessed to have taken part in such a legacy. I speak for my class when I say that we are so grateful for the Malone family's graciousness and hospitality through this whole experience.

Thank you Congressman Walt Minnick for your incredible donation of 300,000 air miles, and more importantly, for your investment in the lives of others.

Thank you United and US Airways for working with the air miles."

These amazingly selfless high school students provided tribute to a complete stranger by going to extreme measures to return a part of his past to his family in the present.

The Helmet was the vehicle.

Honor was the guiding principal.

Love for a stranger was the motivator.

I can almost hear you ask, "Honor makes sense, but why call it "love for a stranger""?

That question forces us to examine ourselves as to why we do what we do.

Are you ready to move from someone else's story to

your own? It may very well take a lot of your energy. So, before we go there, let's take a rest, shall we?

A selah rest.

Chapter 9

Selah Rest:
Love's overpowering strength

As I wrote in my first book, Beautiful Nate, it is vital that readers take a rest when reading books on emotional issues. It's biblical to rest well.

It's called a *selah rest*.

Explaining this more in depth, I quoted this type of *rest* in the following fashion:

"Selah, of course, is the one word used in Psalms to act as a sort of rest for the psalmists or musicians, as they presented key section of Psalms. You probably have seen the word in the Bible and often wondered what it meant.

But there is so much more to the word.

To the Jewish mind, there was no question: The word "Selah" (celah in Hebrew), is an exclamation point of sorts — *stating that the reader, the psalmist, the musician should measure and reflect upon what has been said.*

So, I ask you to take a Selah rest and reflect on what you've read so far and its application to your life — and the lives of those in your family."

That was good advice for *Beautiful Nate.* It's good advice for this book, too.

Love is an incredibly complicated emotion. Its power can overcome the most bitter of emotions that previously occupied a person's heart and mind, when unleashed by God.

God's love liberates people.

That is, if people are willing to listen and reflect on the difficult choices they must make. Selah rest allows the reader to stop and think.

Each of us suffers from the disease of personal selfishness. We don't often call it a disease. Instead we use words that are less offensive while we justify ourselves, our decisions to act *and to not act.* We remain busy about our life, so that we never stop to take a personal inventory.

I am asking you to take that fearless inventory right now.

Think of the vulnerability that has been presented in this book, so far. Who writes a book and openly states that he or she hates their father? Who in the world shakes the family tree to see what falls to the ground? Who reads those sad words of deep dislike about someone else and then includes himself or herself?

As you enter in to think about the things you wish to change about yourself, kick-off your shoes and place your pride on the floor next to them.

How many of us, if we were honest with ourselves, would ever refuse the love of our parents? We might refuse to consciously think about those who have wreaked havoc on hearts - even if they ARE our parents. Haunting memories of yesterday can capture our present time, even as we try to push down those thoughts. The pressure of those thoughts to rise to the surface is often just too great.

Many of us stuff those memories deep into the corners of the basements in our lives. As we exit the homes in which we grew up, we're thankful hearing the front door slam for what we think is the final time.

We leave behind us the life we once lived, hoping it has no influence on the life in front of us.

By thinking in that fashion, we delude ourselves.

Until each of us determines to stop, turn around and re-open that front door, we will never be free of those memories, hurts and hang-ups. Key to that re-examination and revisiting is the need to re-explore forgiveness.

For a number of years I volunteered in our local county jail, being with then-current inmates through a weekly program that was one-part mentoring and two parts Bible study. Others joined me as we worked with those addicted to drugs, criminals convicted of minor and major crimes, robbers and rapists, child molesters and white collar criminals.

Amid all that pain was the occasional moment of laughter.

I hold a funny moment vividly in my memory of meeting a white-collar criminal who was in jail for having stolen an immense amount of money. He had apparently also been involved in politics prior to his incarceration and knew of my work in the political arena, as a candidate and a lobbyist. In jail, he attended a couple of the mid-week events before he summoned up the courage to approach me at the end of one particular evening session. We called our mentoring time "Band of Brothers".

He walked up to me at the end of one of our sessions, as other inmates were ushering out.

"You know who I am," he said matter-of-factly, as if we had previously known one another.

I paused and looked at him.

" I do?" was my only honest response.

"Yeah, of course you do" he responded while looking

from left to right, scanning the limited horizon for any interruptions by another inmate, amid the semi-toothless gaggle of meth-addicted criminals.

"I'm not like the rest of these guys", my new best friend stated flatly.

"You aren't?" I responded. He nodded, no, no, no.

"Come on Dennis, give it a rest, you know who I am," he strongly countered, in a very prideful fashion.

I slowly shook my head back and forth reflecting my confusion, trying as I might to recall if I knew him. I did not.

"How do I handle this?" I asked myself

I suddenly had a perfectly clear God-given opportunity to address this prideful man.

"Oh" I said, "Yeah come to think of it, I DO know who you are!" I said to him a bit louder than how his volume had been toward me. He was now obviously proud that someone whom he felt had political strength and muscle from the outside, would be able in his mind to mentally block out the orange colored jail garb he was wearing and allow him to just be that important person of the past. To be called by his name. To be proud once again.

Wrong conclusion on his part.

I honestly did not know who he was or what he had done — good or bad - on the outside, but I felt this might be a learning moment for him, for others around him and for myself.

I looked him in the eye and emphatically said, "Yeah...you're the guy who lives in this jail, dressed in an orange jumpsuit, along with hundreds of others who stand condemned by the courts. Your value comes not from what you did on the outside, but on who God is making you to be on the inside, my friend. Now go about your business and rest, knowing that God loves you for who you are."

What would be considered a harsh action on the outside of jail was something that this inmate needed to hear. His conman behavior didn't cut it with God, nor with me. He needed to embrace God's love for him. Anything shy of a two-by-four across the face would not have helped him.

It was at this point that he rested, took a fierce inventory of himself and reexamined his life.

Selah rest.

At this point in the book's story are you resting, thinking about the people against whom you have so much hate? Do specific people come to mind? Are you resting well in your life or are you furious every time the name or face of someone who has deeply hurt you crosses your mind?

Are you seeing yourself in any of the situations in any of these chapters?

Convicted? If so, read on. If not, put the book up on a shelf until your life falls in on you — as it will. You'll need the next section then, is my guess.

"Convicted" is a nice Christian term. It's warm and strong at the same time. It implies a tug of the Holy Spirit on you or me in a way vaguely reminiscent of a church campfire ring, or an evangelist's heart-warming story that moves your emotions to give of yourself or our finances.

That's NOT what I'm talking about.

I'm bringing forward for your consideration the concept of a person in jail or prison — a "convict" who was tried, found guilty and sentenced.

Am I one of them? Are you?

If you are a "convict", are you in need of being bailed out?

Let's take a sober look at your life and how you got to where you are today.

Saying goodbye to one's childhood is a good place to start, isn't it?

PAYING TRIBUTE
til
THE END

Chapter 10

Saying Goodbye

We stood together in his bright warm Florida front room; the opaque shadow of death attempting to cross the threshold.

But it was not yet death's time.

The world was still bright.

I gently held his 84-year-old tanned and gracefully aged face in my two cupped hands, looking into the dark brown eyes of the man who gave me life. I was 56 years old.

He stood tall. Military tall with a bearing that seemed always to say "this far and no farther" and yet he allowed me to hold his face in my two hands.

It was early April and I'd been with my father, Bill, and stepmother, Marilyn, and a care-taking grandson, Paul Ruth, in their lovely Florida home for 4 days. Joining me over those days were my college son, my youngest brother and a sister, along with her loved ones. The surprise visit was ending.

Many had already headed to their homes.

Soon it was just my brother my dad and me in a brilliantly sun-lit front room.

And it was time to leave, forever.

My father's cancer had taken a turn for the worse and the next step was clear. He would be dead within 4 months, my brother, an RN, told me.

So, I cupped his face in my hands and looked into his eyes.

"Dad, I will never see you again, this side of Heaven." I said.

He nodded and looked seriously into my eyes and into my heart. His voice was strong, clear and commanding as he slowly shook his head in an affirming way. "I know, bud", he said. "Bud" - He'd always called his sons by the nickname with which his dad had favored him.

I continued, "Thank you for being my father … and for being one of my best friends." I choked up. Words became constricted deep in my throat. They were unable to find air and express themselves as sounds.

"I know", he said again, this time a little softer — still nodding his head in an understanding old man-ish way. "I love you, bud," he said again. I think my brothers and I always enjoyed him calling us that. A little gift, I'm sure, from *his own* father to him, then to us and finally to our own sons.

And I teared up. "I love you too, Pop", I said. It was an affectionate nickname that I'd started calling him a few years ago. Strangely, it was the same name he called his own father. How fitting that it had become a recent addition to my vocabulary.

For the first 39 years of my life I had not cared for my father; and those types of words were not sentiments I had employed in conversations with him.

Not at all.

I was a self-focused son of the 50's and 60's; my dad was a father of the 40's — tough and unyielding. He'd lived through the depression, WWII and Korea. I'd barely begun to live. Compared to his life, my life seemed soft and selfish. You'd never hear such words as a result of my adolescent attitude, though.

I'd wanted my father's love since boyhood and yet at the same time had equally and passionately begun to hate my father as I grew older when that love was not returned according to my expectations.

Yet, now at the end, things were different.

Recently, different words came forward from him to me; words like *I love you, how are you doing?, can you come to see us?* All words, questions and sentences that were never uttered until a change of profound magnitude happened in both our lives, taking us far away from the burning-red recesses of hatred and on into a world of peace and joy, which we had never known before.

On this April day in 2012 I no longer even had an ounce of hated in me for the man who raised me.

And my love for him overwhelmed me to the point I could not speak.

Having prayed for far too long as a child that my dad would die, now with tears, I faced his death. My dad would be dead in less than four months. My heart was crushing within me.

What changed me?

What interrupted a life of hatred for my father and exchanged in its place the deepest of love?

Forgiveness and honor.

Bill Mansfield died on July 30th, 2012, while I was finishing the writing of this book. I hadn't expected his death to even be a part of this larger story. In a fitting way, though, my dad's death brought a proper completion to the story.

You hold in your hand a story that transcends the death of one man as well as moving past the tale of his son, the author. This story is *for* you, it may even be a story *of* you. It's a chance to consider the interwoven elements of *your* own life, examining the unmet expectations of *your* story, subtlety cajoling you to ask yourself profound questions about the people in your life who have held you back, hurt you, used you and discarded you as though you had little value. It may well become a tale of self-discovery.

My custom, over the last 27 years is to spend a portion of each summer on Catalina Island, just off the coast of Southern California, in Gallagher Cove at a little camp called Campus by The Sea (CBS). It's a place of beauty and of rest. I've written two books there.

It was while on that island that my bride, Susan, received word of my dad's death. She was charged with the duty of telling me. Gently and kindly she relayed the terribly difficult and yet not-unexpected news to me.

I stood for a second, hearing her words — even understanding the loss now before me — and was *momentarily* quiet, standing on a veranda at CBS, while leaning on a banister that parallels the thick wood steps which bring guests up from the rocky beachfront and the sea.

It was only a momentary quiet.

Then bellows of sadness rolled through my insides, crashing immediately and irregularly against me, inside and out. I found myself gutted at the midsection, leaning over the banister, staring at the ground some fifteen feet below me. I wept the tears of family loss, of father loss. Uncaring who heard me I cried out as tears gushed up from my deep well. I had no control over myself, nor did I care about being in control.

My dad was dead. He was gone.

The man I had uncaringly prayed would die when I was young was *now* dead. It was so painfully and ironically true.

And my bride allowed me to just simply and deeply sob.

I'd learned with the premature death of my oldest son Nate, at age 27, that tears must come, turning themselves to torrents, if needs be.

And it is always *"needs be"*. I've chronicled that jarring life-death experience in my work, *Beautiful Nate*. I was changed to the core by that experience.

"How now would the death of my dad change me?" I wondered.

The sudden plans of long travel began; a trip across the nation to mourn the passing of my parent. Those who have done so know exactly what sentiments arise at moments like this. Those who have not yet experienced such an odd mix of traveling sadness *and* calm will most likely *in time* face such chaotic times. It is like planning a wedding in three days, my son's funeral director told me 3+ years prior. He was right.

Nine children, many more grandchildren and a sprinkling of great-grand children stopped the activities of August and hurried in masse by plane or car from many different regional locations in the U.S. to Florida.

It's hard to explain and describe the change in appearance of any person stricken with cancer. For my dad the period from April to August was drastic. The ravages of cancer seem only to come in second place to the greater and needful poisoning of the flesh accepted and demanded by chemotherapy.

In April, Dad was still strong and solid, especially for a man whose 84-and-a-half birthday we celebrated. While with him in April, my son, Colin, flew down from his sophomore studies at the US Military Academy, West Point. It is the custom upon graduation from West Point that cadets ask a key military mentor to "pin on" the newly received 2nd Lieutenant's bars. Such were the plans of both grandfather and grandson for May 2014. Now cancer had intruded and two years were left before that event could occur.

Colin and I talked about a suitable substitute, given the gravity of the pending visit.

He was less than a month away from becoming a Junior (or Cow, in West Point vernacular) and would be exchanging under-classmen brass for upper class brass and new responsibilities. Retired Chief Master Sergeant William E. Mansfield might just be the NCO to pin on West Point Cadet Mansfield's upper class brass.

With a flurry of surprise and an afternoon of delight a band of brothers and sisters, wife and grandkids collected "the old man", re-uniformed him in his US Air Force blues with service medals, shined shoes with a snappy garrison cap, with which to top it all off. He joined my son, attired in his West Point summer uniform for the ceremony.

It was breathtaking in many ways.

My father's hometown of Panama City Beach, Florida has an elegantly simple Veteran's Park, replete with floor pavers bearing its city's military residents by name, rank and wartime in which they served. In the center of the park stand several flagpoles in a relatively tight circle, each flying the flag of one of a different service. At the base of each flagpole stands embedded in concrete adjacent to the pavers several corresponding podium-sized monuments — one for each of the services.

We stood next to the US Army podium-monument in solemn assembly.

Though my dad arrived seated slumped on an electric scooter, his military bearing took command as he stopped the vehicle, looked around for a place to stand and then raised himself from it. Before our eyes, this 84-year-old father and grandfather regained his rank, regained his strength and stood at attention.

Chief Master Sergeant Bill Mansfield was now in the area.

Although I had initially planned to act as MC for this event, *the Chief* would have none of it. He took control of the event from the start and would not relinquish it till we were done. For a glimmering time period, this very man issued the challenge to a West Point grandson, honored him with a new upper-class rank and commissioned him into the profession of arms, as only he could do.

Then, as if on cue both grandson and grandfather pivoted to their right, turning to the huge United States flag in the center of the memorial and without a word immediately stood at attention, snapping identically perfect salutes. They held their salutes in muted respect for one another, for those who had also served and for the nation.

Other than at his own military retirement ceremony 46 years before, this was my father's high-water mark for service to the nation: he was officially passing the torch to his progeny, represented here by one of many grandsons who now served. While he was alive he never wore that uniform again.

Four months later, as he laid in state for the family viewing he was in uniform once and for all. His would be a military funeral with complete honors.

Strangely, at the funeral, I felt his impression but not his spirit. Bill Mansfield was gone.

In an intimate time together prior to the service and with the help of a pastor, my siblings and I spoke among ourselves of his imprint on us; one sister spoke of how he taught her poetry, another spoke of him as a complex man, still a third sister remembered his singing at church — how beautiful and powerful his voice was, a brother could only say one phrase — "he was Dad", I spoke of his leadership, another sister spoke of his story telling, a brother and two sisters spoke of his patriotism.

Yet it was his wife, Marilyn, who put it simply: "he was a loving man who loved his children, grandchildren and his pets."

His own last words were shared to his loving bride were probably the most poignant expressed: "We've had a good life together." And they did.

My own final words about my dad were spoken through soft tears of missing him.

I shared how when I left West Point prior to my third year, due to a poor academic performance, he simply said "They don't deserve you. Come home."

He was the man I hated most when I lived under his roof and yet at the lowest point of my then-young life, he bid me return to him.

I eventually came home to my dad. It was long journey of many years, but I came home to my dad and my friend.

It can only happen when we allow honor, hope and

forgiveness to interweave themselves in our lives.

And sometimes they come to us when we least expect it. Like when we receive a gift.

Chapter 11

Unfinished Business

I wrote what follows on the morning after my father died, while I was on Catalina Island, off the coast of Southern California:

"With my father's passing I've thought about the type of man he was.

In fact, I stated that I would place "more" about him at some point when he was first sick. That point has just simply eluded me.

Each time I opened the laptop, my spirit closed... and I was unable to cogently place a clear thought on the compose page.

Until this morning.

I'm headed by boat into the City of Avalon, on Catalina Island. Each Wednesday the camp my wife and I are volunteering at brings the staff and campers together on a boat and after a two mile boat ride, we dock at the Pleasure Pier, disembark and spend a delightful day in this lovely island coastal city.

It's the city where my father spent his honeymoon, 37 years ago this next week. He and my stepmother, Marilyn, flew to Catalina Island and began their life together, "26 miles across the sea". That fact inspired me to write.

Dad's life was a complex one. Most of our lives fall into that category, I suppose, but Bill Mansfield's life was indeed that - to the degree that I could see it, as his third-born of seven.

I begin my brief thoughts by saying this: we can never really know our fathers and mothers. We can think we do, but our position as a child disallows us the proper balanced perspective to do so. The mere fact that we begin our lives as babies, totally dependent on them, hour by hour, day by day places them on a god-like level to the little mini-me that abides within us, long after we achieve adult status.

Our parents are simply too big to comprehend, for many years. Then, suddenly, they shrink.

I mean, really shrink - really quickly. Our adolescence falsely builds us up at the expense of tearing them down. Angry back talking combines with surly attitudes to distance the "cool" us from the "stupid" them.

Often we see our parents for the deficits they have in their own lives. I saw them plentifully in Bill Mansfield. I began to detest him. And I enjoyed it.

How terribly sad. How terribly normal. How terribly unneeded. That was the case for my dad, Bill, and me.

Mom and I had very little tough times.

Dad? Too many to count. Too painful to recollect. Too corrosive to capture.

And it never got better.

Until I was 39 years old.

My bride and I had been married for 18 years at that moment and our life had gone its own way, only occasionally touching my Dad and Step mom's world. Only when absolutely necessary. Why embrace fire, I thought. I had moved on.

But not really. My bride saw it in me - the corrosive acid was leaking out of its container onto everyone. Especially on to my kids and my sweet wife.

And we'd be putting him up over Father's Day weekend.

Words cannot fully capture what happened to Bill and Dennis Mansfield after I completed the reading.

It was as if God came down into that dining room and healed us. Both of us. In an instant. In a twinkling of an eye.

And no one was more surprised than I was. Not even my Dad. He was hoping for reconciliation with his child. All parents do hope for that. And it happened.

Susan and my kids were eyewitnesses to the change of heart, the love expressed, the ability to speak openly and the ability to receive criticism. God's hand had cleansed us.

And we were better men for it - for the next 17 years. Dad became one of my best friends. Forgiveness can do that to two men, I found.

I saw him for the last time in April. We talked regularly, until Monday, July 30th, when Dad entered into the arms of the Savior who healed us.

And so I return to Avalon today. To think of Dad. To thank God for having given him to me as my father.

And to thank the Lord for changing my own heart."

These were the first words I wrote as an orphan.

That's a strange way to put it in my 57th year of age. But it was true. I'd lost my mother in 1994 when she was 69 years old, and now I just lost my father, as he crested the 6-month mark of being 84 years of age.

Both my dad and mom were no longer there. They no longer represented the link to my childhood. The two people who saw me almost every day of my childhood could not reflect on those days when I needed counsel. They who created me were now with their Creator.

It was a subtle unveiling of becoming an orphan, but fully real, nonetheless.

And I remember asking myself in an odd, almost embarrassing way, "Ok, is it now my moment to fully be an adult?" The answer of course was that I had been an adult for a very long period of time, yet somewhere in each of us lives a 10 year old kid who so wants his or her parents' approval and love, who can't wait to run home to tell mom what happened at school today or who so fully needs to seek advice on some financial matter or marriage concern.

I was alive as a son while my father was dead; he'd soon only be noticed as some great grand child's' ancestor in some type of permanent past. But *today*, he was not there. He could no longer be there *today*.

Amid the rush of time and emotions by all my siblings and me, our combined families were preparing to fly to his funeral with very mixed feelings. I could understand these feelings, given the history I'd had with my dad — that we all had had with our dad.

And yet my emotions were singular: I was sad that my friend had died. I loved him for the last almost two decades of our lives as though he was a best friend — for in fact he was. I saw Dad's other adult children and grand children arrive with me at the house that he and my stepmom, Marilyn, have enjoyed for years in Panama City Beach Florida. I walked over the threshold of the house's front door and immediately felt his loss. The often warm and yet booming voice was gone. No hug, no kiss greeted us as we walked in - not until we met our stepmom.

I remembered how four short months ago, I'd knocked on the door and my dad greeted me with the hug of a man who loved his son. He was strong, clear thinking and so hospitable. Though his health and mental state began to show raw edges, my brother, Ken, my sister Joyce, her family, my son, Colin and I enjoyed our overall time with him. A month or so later, other siblings came to see him and say good-bye, too.

Four months later all my siblings and many of our children and grandchildren arrived at his home to say the official farewell of mourning. Hours blended into experiences. I walked around his house and wrote notes to myself, just simply to capture the visual sense that my father had existed. His house said that he was still there. We all knew differently.

My notes read in part:
- Monday, August 6th, 2012 — Sunday was a long day of travel from LAX to Ft. Walton Beach, FL
- My brand new grand daughter slept in a bureau drawer last night! Ha, what a strange thing to become a memory. Dad would have laughed.
- Walking in the house showed us a much tidier version of what we'd seen in April. Dad was a bit of an organized pack rat. Everything in order — just a lot of everything!
- The conversation flowed freely.
- I stepped into Dad's bedroom. I saw his US Air Force garrison cap, I saw his Boise State hat!
- I looked at his efficient drawer and desk set up. It all looked like Dad.

• Strangely, I felt his impression but not his spirit.

• I spoke with my step mom, Marilyn, about how my dad died. She told me.

• I stood where his hospital bed had been — the bed from which he left this earth and entered Heaven. I looked up at the ceiling and then imagined looking down at the bed, as well as the entire room, as he must have upon his exit. It was powerful.

When the actual funeral occurred, I pulled out my pen and paper and wrote copious notes and impressions. It was my way of capturing the events of that special day before they would fade from my memory.

I watched my siblings — 7 of us by birth, 2 more by marriage to our step mom. All interacted well with each other, all were dealing with the loss of their father as each one should. All chose to love their father, many had a hard time liking him. Again, I understood that.

Scripture was everywhere, for Dad had pressed into the Lord in the last several years of his life. John 14 was spoken by the pastor, telling us to not let our hearts be troubled. Romans 8 was quoted asking us "who would separate us from the love of God?" John 11 reminded us of Jesus love for his dear friend who had died, Lazarus. Jesus wept for his friend's death. We were told that we could weep for our father's death. Some did. Others couldn't, though they had wept for years when he was alive. I wept because I loved him and because I missed him. I wept because, upon entering Heaven he was greeted by the booming voice of my son Nate, with a hug and a kiss.

The unfinished business of adult children and grand children appeared to be brought to Bill Mansfield's funeral. Each said goodbye as they had normally said hello for years. Some deeply pensive, others somewhat shallow, still others hoping to glean a final morsel of food for their starved souls. Dad couldn't give it to them, not in life and certainly not in death.

I remembered back to my '67 Austin Healy Sprite and the following conversation I had with my dad at the very dinner where our hearts were reconnected on Father's Day 1995. Since the walls had tumbled down, no subject was off-limits, so I forged ahead.

"Dad, for years I've been angry at you for something. May I share it with you in hopes of clearing it up and reconciling?" He nodded in hearty approval.

"Well, Dad, when I went away to West Point, I left my convertible sports car at home. When I returned from the Army, my car was gone. Why did you take it and sell it without even asking me?" My tone was civil, my heart was honest. I'd carried this hurt in my heart for a long time. The very gift he gave me in such a wonderful moment when I was in high school was taken away from me under the cover of darkness, while I was away at college.

"What are you talking about, Denny?" he asked.

We both looked at each other.

"Don't you remember that before you left for West Point, you and your high school girlfriend were stopped at a light on Lark Ellen Street in West Covina preparing to turn left when a giant trash hauler turned too quickly and ran over the front of that beautiful car, squashing the engine? You barely were able to tuck your legs in time, before the wheels went over the hood. Remember?"

As he was saying these very words, a complete and instant picture of the accident raced forward from my memory to the forefront of my thoughts. I DID remember it! He had to have the car towed away at the cost of over $100, it was a complete wreck, unsalvageable.

I had carried this vain imagination in my mind for 21 years. And suddenly I was free of its pull on me. I had to laugh, as well. Had I been my dad at such an "aha" moment as we were experiencing, I would have then asked my adult child, "so are you going to pay me back for the towing charge?" But he missed his opportunity....ha.

Forgiveness had even occurred as a result of the vain imagination's grip being released.

From my experience, through honoring and forgiving him, I realized that he could never give me anything that I demanded. Forgiveness is the only thing that once given, gives back even more.

I had to give something to him, instead. Giving, after all, was his love language.

Honor was the needed gift. And I gave it. Most importantly, he received it

Chapter 12

Hate's Consuming Fire

Wrestling with forgiveness — why give it?

Say it loud, say it clear
You can listen as well as you hear
It's too late when we die
To admit we don't see eye to eye
In the Living Years. - Mike & the Mechanics

The haunting lyrics of this resonating melody speak of anger, fear and dying. Mostly, though, the well-crafted lyrics express an intensity of a quiet and consuming hatred.

I know a bit about hate. Not just because I learned how to hate my own father, though I did, but because I learned how others came to hate me.

It doesn't have to be about your father.

While in politics, I was a state leader in the national pro-family movement begun by Focus on the Family's Dr. James Dobson. I founded a non-profit lobbying entity that worked in association with Focus on the Family. I've written extensively about that time in my book *Beautiful Nate* and do not need to expand on it here, except to say that some people REALLY did not like me. And in many instances, I gave them reason to. It was a case of me wanting to upset my opponents — and I succeeded.

A little bit ago I wrote a piece about the use of fear and anger in politics. It tapped into those years and opens the door to seeing how arrogance, anger and near-hatred, though successful in political races and public policy issues, makes for a life un-lived.

I wrote,

"Politics, in its rawest form, is the governing of our own small city blocks.

We care about how crime impacts people and places "out there". However, if we are honest with others, and ourselves, we REALLY care how crime impacts our own neighbor next door...or more specifically, ourselves. Don't we?

Selfish or selfless? Hmmm... probably both.

Americans seem to be wondering out loud as to whether the formally-ever-present "thin blue line of civility" can actually protect our kids and us. Will the police really show up?

And fear seems to be gripping us more and more.

So, therefore the politics of fear seem to be the most "use-able" form of governance. Whether in a small neighborhood store… or in an editorial about how a governor or president is failing in his duties to "protect" the schools or the students or the older people; fear…is everywhere.

But is that fear-based way of influencing people REALLY legitimate? We know it works, but is it legitimate? Is it needed and will it work for the best interests of the community?

I have worked with drug addicts and alcoholics for a number of years. They're convicted criminals and then they become ex-inmates. Though there are others who are far more knowledgeable than I am in dealing with this demographic, my experience over these years shows me that crime committed by drug addicts has everything to do with stealing things and nothing to do with hurting people physically. Yes, the angry sociopaths exist…but far more in the films we watch than in the lives we lead.

Losing things to a thief is hard to deal with. We feel violated, don't we? But do we REALLY need to live lives of always digging moats around our properties and our families? That could be the harder question to answer.

Many citizens are fearful of almost everything: losing their jobs, losing their security, losing their financial cushion. They are afraid and WANT something on which to focus that fear.

And so, at times, a spirit of fear-based banding together blossoms.

The balance in this equation is as follows: there must be NO vigilante-ism by folks or any others desiring to serve their neighborhoods. Protecting their families, yes! Pretending to be peace officers? No.

Being fearful of fear helps no one."

Fear is the gasoline that's poured on the embers of hatred to ignite consuming fires in individuals, neighborhoods and whole regions of the nation.

In many people's lives, the consuming fires of personal animosity start as responses to what they perceive as personal affronts. A slight here, an unintended glance there — these very small and seemingly unimportant acts of unintended unkindness take a toll on the person who fails to forgive.

Peter Gozdeck of San Diego, is the man who mentored me in business and in my faith when I was a relatively new Christian. Both in good business practices and in a well-balanced life, Peter had an expression that stayed with me and guides my life today: "Keep short accounts," Peter would instruct me. Whether it was the accounts payable debt that my then-company owed or the accounts receivable income that was owed to my company, the goal was always to limit the amount of time between when an amount was owed and when it was paid. Long periods between those two points caused nothing put heartache and pain for one or both parties.

Peter explained that life was like that, too.

The pain of people hurting us creates something "owed" in our relationship with them. Like funds put away in a savings account, we tend to store up the anger that accompanies the pain. The politically correct world of niceness in which many of us live tends to dismiss honest interplay and disagreement between individuals as though it is really mean-spirited behavior.

And as that happens, people's anger increases yet is stored away.

Writing a book of one's own life can create a delicate balance. We all tend to want to be judged by our intentions, while we judge every one else by their actions, don't we?

While the book you hold in your hands is my story, it also involves the lives of others. I've learned some rich truth from preparing such a vulnerable book about honor and tribute in my own life: things aren't always what they seem.

People's passionate emotions offer justified housing and a comfort zone for their anger and bitterness.

How about if we change the pronouns from theirs to ours; from them to us?

Maybe even closer to home - from us to me?

A bit painful? More than a bit.

While finishing Finding Malone, I attended my 35th Class Reunion at The United States Military Academy, West Point. The Academy is a majestic collection of medieval-looking buildings standing atop an outcrop of land first dedicated as a fort by General George Washington for its strategic significance.

Key to West Point's strategic long term history is the Cadet Honor Code which states " A cadet will not lie, cheat, steal or tolerate those who do."

I was honored to be voted President of my class – upon graduation it is a position established for life. Each class of cadets enters together on a set day during Beast Barracks (West Point's boot camp). They stay together all four years and graduate together.

The class of 1978 holds a unique place in the Academy's history for two reasons. First, during our sophomore year, many in the junior class above us participated in the largest cheating scandal in the history of West Point. Hundreds and hundreds were indicted, many were found guilty. Of those who were found guilty, some were separated from the academy and over a hundred were "turned back" into my class. The military chain of command saw value in these cadets and allowed them to stay.

They were folded into my class, graduating with my friends.

But not with me.

The Dean didn't like my penchant for poor grades in higher math and saw fit to separate me just prior to the junior year; a year in which my classmates would soon be mixed with those who had been found guilty of not adhering to the honor code.

Those young men cheated and returned to graduate. I didn't cheat and graduated from a different university. The second reason for uniqueness? Upon my departure, my class voted for a new Class President, Les Szabolcsi.

I embraced a consuming anger inside me for a few years against those who asked me to leave. Injustice and unfairness fed that anger. But not for too many years...

In time, I began to see the fuller wisdom of the Dean's actions – I was no engineer, I was no Army officer-to-be. I enjoyed politics and focused my professional life on public service, rather than military service. Les was an Airborne Ranger even before he arrived at the Academy. He fit.

At our 35th Reunion, I saw original classmates briefly mention those who had been grandfathered into our class – it was done with honor, with graciousness and never with a hint of judgment. As I witnessed such honoring behavior I was thankful that the consuming anger that had once owned me – and most probably had once owned those young men who had cheated – no longer was a part of my life. I was free.

And we each write our own story, don't we? Each of us has the chance to be free.

One's own story tends to capture all the "facts" while at the time deftly discounting all the emotions of others. We often so deceive ourselves that as we each author our own life, we forget to research other people's perspectives. It's understandable. And it's unkind to ourselves, in the long run.

Though I knew better, the consuming fire that I felt during many of my personal losses, including this college blip, was actually burning me. Like holding coals in my hand to throw at others, the degree of burn and pain became my injury, not others.

So how did I extinguish the fire?

I did it through forgiveness. Not for others' sake but for my own.

Though it was one of the hardest things I could do as a young man, I forgave myself and others and sought ways that I could be a blessing, rather than a curse. I did so in the power of Christ, because my own power was so limited.

Wrestling with forgiveness is a very difficult thing to do. Every part of us that cries out for justice for others, will if provided the opportunity, demand mercy for ourselves. The success in employing the act of forgiving another person is in realizing that mercy must be applied to all of us, because justice is only God's to mete out.

Like an offender whom you embrace and take into your life, and that of your family, only to be dishonored and set upon in all manner of anger and horrible actions and words, honor and tribute must STILL remain the order of the day.

Bruce Wilkinson writes in his deeply moving book, You were Born for This, (J)ust like the king in Jesus' story, God gets angry when those He has forgiven everything refuse to forgive each other for comparable trifles...He does turn people over to the painful consequences of their own unforgiveness."

These principles can only be obtained through the purposeful act of forgiving.

In the classic work, Les Miserables (1862), Chapter 11, "The Bishop Works", the author Victor Hugo penned it this way:

"Ah! here you are!" he exclaimed, looking at Jean Valjean. "I am glad to see you. Well, but how is this? I gave you the candlesticks too, which are of silver like the rest, and for which you can certainly get two hundred francs. Why did you not carry them away with your forks and spoons?"

Jean Valjean opened his eyes wide, and stared at the venerable Bishop with an expression which no human tongue can render any account of.

"Monseigneur," said the brigadier of gendarmes, "so what this man said is true, then? We came across him. He was walking like a man who is running away. We stopped him to look into the matter. He had this silver--"

"And he told you," interposed the Bishop with a smile, "that it had been given to him by a kind old fellow of a priest with whom he had passed the night? I see how the matter stands. And you have brought him back here? It is a mistake."

"In that case," replied the brigadier, "we can let him go?"

"Certainly," replied the Bishop.

The gendarmes released Jean Valjean, who recoiled.

"Is it true that I am to be released?" he said, in an almost inarticulate voice, and as though he were talking in his sleep.

"Yes, thou art released; dost thou not understand?" said one of the gendarmes.

"My friend," resumed the Bishop, "before you go, here are your candlesticks. Take them."

He stepped to the chimney-piece, took the two silver candlesticks, and brought them to Jean Valjean. The two women looked on without uttering a word, without a gesture, without a look which could disconcert the Bishop.

Jean Valjean was trembling in every limb. He took the two candlesticks mechanically, and with a bewildered air.

"Now," said the Bishop, "go in peace. By the way, when you return, my friend, it is not necessary to pass through the garden. You can always enter and depart through the street door. It is never fastened with anything but a latch, either by day or by night."

Then, turning to the gendarmes:--"You may retire, gentlemen."

The gendarmes retired.

Jean Valjean was like a man on the point of fainting.

The Bishop drew near to him, and said in a low voice:-- "Do not forget, never forget, that you have promised to use this money in becoming an honest man."

Jean Valjean, who had no recollection of ever having promised anything, remained speechless. The Bishop had emphasized the words when he uttered them. He resumed with solemnity:--

"Jean Valjean, my brother, you no longer belong to evil, but to good. It is your soul that I buy from you; I withdraw it from black thoughts and the spirit of perdition, and I give it to God."

Chapter 13

Honor, hope and forgiveness

I have a friend, Chad Estes, who has known me for many years. Chad is a former pastor, a current blogger and an amazing professional photographer. His eye, his camera and his laptop keyboard create a mix of mercy and new wine through the feelings he captures in word and image.

In the early years of his pastorate, he didn't really like me. My guess is that I probably gave him many reasons to feel that way. I eventually changed.

In time he didn't even like being a pastor, either. He eventually changed.

He liked the new wine of the Good News but the old wineskin wasn't working for him any longer.

Then losses came into my life *and* his. Business challenges happened for me; he was let go in his job from a large church. Political defeats became commonplace for me; spiritual defeats for him. In one sense they were bad times for both of us, in another sense they became the best times of our lives, because they changed us.

Chad and I became close friends. Not that Chad was waiting for me to be swallowed up by my losses; he's far too kind for that. It's just that his own defeats and brokenness gave him much more compassion for others, like me. I grew in compassion for him, as well.

So, in 2010 when all my political and business aspirations had crashed and burned, when the business I ran, ran into the ground, I was pleasantly surprised to be greeted by two other friends. They invited me to join them as they proposed a possible eleventh-hour campaign to help a tired U.S. Congressional candidate who had no chance of winning.

His name was Raul Labrador and he was going to lose his bid for the GOP nomination for Congress, unless people helped him.

Mr. Labrador had only about 40 days or so left, before voters cast their ballots in the GOP nomination during the primary election of May, 2010. He was opposed by a much better financed and widely endorsed candidate. All signals pointed to defeat.

Where a decade before, I had been a highly favored candidate for this same Congressional seat in the US House of Representatives, now I was asked to be Mr. Labrador's Campaign Spokesman. I'd be a part of the team that ran a relatively short guerilla-style social media campaign. It would be a wild ride for 40 days.

On the night of the primary election, Chad Estes asked me if he could accompany my bride, Susan, my son, Colin and me to the election night festivities to view the results. I was honored to have him join us.

Unlike the results of a decade before in my own race, Raul Labrador won the election in an upset and went on to be elected as one of Idaho's U. S. Congressmen. He has since become a national leader interviewed by all the major media leaders.

On the evening of the successful primary election, Chad wrote an unintended "Tribute" to me that, though brief in length, is deep in meaning and history. When I first read it, I was alone. There was no barbeque spread on a table, there was no movie that I'd just watched with loved ones. It was just me, alone. And yet the impact of the tribute that I extended to my dad *all those years ago* was returned to me by my friend in just a few words.

May each of you actively look for the reconciliation, hope, honor and forgiveness about which Chad writes. May we gently reach into the lives of others, whether they deserve it or not, honoring them with their own tributes, freeing ourselves (and maybe even them, too) by a clear act of forgiveness.

Here is the tribute Chad Estes wrote for me:

"I keep an eye open for reconciliation—mostly in the area of relationships. I have several, important stories to share about God healing relationships between others and

me, especially when I had given up trying. I'm still looking for his hand in the broken relationships I have that appear beyond salvage.

Tonight I had the pleasure of seeing a mix of redemption and reconciliation for one of my friends. Dennis Mansfield ran for the 1st Congressional Seat of Idaho a decade ago. It was supposed to be his moment in the sun but it ended in a painful and personal defeat.

However, what others meant for evil God intended for other purposes. There has been a lot of pain and a lot of progress in this last ten years. But tonight there was a present to unwrap—I watched Dennis in the same hotel, the same big convention room, working on the same congressional race as his defeat years ago.

This time it was different—he was helping someone else reach their dreams, he didn't seem all that wrapped up in winning (I kept tabs on the numbers more than he did), and his identity wasn't centered in what other people thought of him. I watched and listened to him walk around the room, not as a crafty politician, but as a man who cares about people, character, and his family. The turnaround tonight was beautiful on so many levels.

I'm not convinced that God has picked one political party over another, or that he's casting the winning vote in our primaries. But this, however, I'm thoroughly convinced of— Papa is especially fond of Dennis!"

My father and my father-in-law both showered me with kind words at the success of that 2010 GOP

Primary win in Idaho and yet, as Chad said, it was my Papa in Heaven whose smile was the widest, I think.

Thank you for being with me through the journey of this book.

In finding Malone you saw how I found so much more in my own life.

My hope is that you will also find a new part of yourself. My guess is you probably already have.

This has been the true story of a father and son overcoming *un*expressed love, deep personal disappointment and ultimately hatred, through a series of unplanned-for acts of intentional honor - and the subsequent restored hope and fresh forgiveness that came as a result, healing their relationship and bringing them together as best friends for the last 18 years of the father's life.

May it be an example of honor and healing for the painful things that face you in your life.

Remember, the best is yet to come.

Appendix

B ill Mansfield's letter to Mrs. Malone
February 2009

"Dear Mrs. Malone,

In early December 1971 I went to Selfridge Air Force Base commissary, just outside Mt. Clemens, Michigan to do my weekly grocery shopping for my large-sized family and after doing same and putting it all in the car, I heard laughter from nearby in the parking lot and being the nosey one that I am, I went over to see what was going on. Fun was going on… a bazaar was in full steam… people picking up this and then that… putting old hats and/or scarves on their heads and bodies… posing like "this is the rage, or what?"… and the crowd would become hysterical… then they would auction the items being shown to the highest bidder. It was fun!

Eventually, before my ice cream melted in the car… a fellow posed in a World War I army outfit. It was pretty raggedy and didn't do too good in the bidding. I remember they held up this dirty old helmet and asked for $2.99… nobody bid on it… then for one reason or another I got to thinking about my son, Dennis, and how he liked odd things and Christmas was nearing and that I could clean up for him.

Someone else in the audience must have had the same thought, re his son and yelled "One dollar"… I offered up "One dollar seventy five cents!"… the other fellow chickened out and I went home and cleaned up my treasure! While doing so, I noticed a name printed inside it. My wife, a

WWII Marine Corps Sergeant didn't think my selection was
a very wise Christmas present, but I prevailed on the subject."
* – William E. Mansfield, Florida*

DennisMansfield.com
December 21, 2008
A.J. Malone: A tale of 12 Idaho high school students and
a WWI helmet
The name A.J. Malone may mean very little to you.
It meant nothing to my students in an International His-
tory course I teach at the Vineyard's home school coop.
Until they saw his helmet...a vintage 1917 US Army
helmet...the kind they wore before Pearl Harbor happened.
There, written on the leather bindings inside the helmet
was his name: A.J. Malone. A silent name of the helmet's
one time owner.
The kids began an internet quest to find out if Mr. Malone
had served in WWI....or was even alive today.
And they found out about him. Yes, the helmet was made
in 1917 but its owner never received it until he went into
the US army on February 2nd 1941 - a helmet 24 years in
storage, never used in the First World War, but soon to see
action in the Second one.
They then began the quest of finding the family of Mr.
Malone....through the internet, emails and phone calls,
this past week they found the Malone family and began
the delicate work of letting his family know of their desire
to return this helmet that spanned two world wars...to its
owner's family.
They have a Facebook account, named after A.J. Malone,
they have mounds of paper and research data on his Fort
and his Company and his travels.
Now they want to meet a family member and return

the helmet (an antique hunters dream) for free. They have invited the family to choose a member to come to Idaho to receive the helmet...and these high school kids are willing to find a way to fly him/her out for the event, plus a hotel and meals.

What a story. I hope it comes to pass.

Den

PS: My dad gave me this helmet for Christmas 1971 and I have had it in storage off-and-on since then. I had it through West Point and through my political life. A silent reminder of "somebody else" who served. It took my wife, a teacher, to ask me about the name on the bindings....and now a whole school is ready to help reconnect a piece of one soldier's military life with his family, these 37 years since I was given it - a full 67 years since he first received it.

DennisMansfield.com

February 10, 2009

Congressman Minnick comes through for the kids. US Airways and United Airlines make a way, too.

I've had quite a few people ask me for an update on the Vineyard's High School 11th graders who are trying to get to CT to give back a WWII helmet to the widow and family of A.J. Malone of Middletown, CT - a vet who served America at Normandy, Sicily and N. Africa as a medic. Well, guess what?

US Congressman Walt Minnick, newbie freshman from ID who recently defeated my long-time friend, Congressman Bill Sali, stepped forward. He helped me and he helped my students, though I never helped him.

No kidding.

Walt heard about the need of the kids...and provided 300,000 frequent flier miles to have tickets available for

the students and chaperones.
The Vineyard team of teens is going to CT...next Wednesday.

US Airways and United Airlines joined the Congressman to ensure that this bulk of miles would be converted to current tickets. - a wonderful honor to the kids, the family and to the memory of A.J. Malone.

If you are not familiar with this story, please Facebook "A.J. Malone" or Google " WWII helmet, A.J. Malone, Anthony Malone and gift" on my site (up above) and learn. It is the story of encouragement and of love of a veteran, long ago having served and only 8 years removed from having passed away. It is a story of young men and women who would not give up! Both during WWII and in 2009.

And now they are going. They have no money, will be sleeping on floors and will be flying by the kindness of a stranger...to honor a veteran. They leave Wednesday, February 18th and will honor the Malone family on Friday, February 20th.

All because of a WWII helmet and a dream.
Amazing.
Den

Feb 20, 2009 Blog by Students
Monday, February 23, 2009
The legacy lives on

What an incredible trip!

Thinking back on this entire experience, I am blown away by all the opportunities, experiences, and miracles that have taken place. I am positive that God's hand has been on this trip from the very beginning. The legacy of A.J. Malone is an incredible one, and I feel so honored and blessed to have taken part in such a legacy. I speak for my class when I say that we are so grateful for the Malone family's graciousness and hospitality through this whole experience, and on last week's trip itself. Thanks to all of our host families from the New Haven Vineyard. Your kindness has NOT gone unnoticed! Enjoy that Idaho candy. Thank you Sara Elander for all you did for our class. Your hospitality, joy, and smiles brought warmth where there might have been stress. Thank you Congressman Walt Minnick for your incredible donation of 300,000 air miles, and more importantly, your investment in the lives of others. Thank you United and US Airways for working with the air miles, and for great flights to and from Connecticut. :D

Finally, thank you Mr. Mansfield for EVERYTHING. You've shown this class that given enough prayer, sweat, and blood anything is possible. We have learned so much, and it wouldn't have been possible without you.

I'm sure there are others who deserve thanking, and indeed my class does thank everyone who contributed in any way to this trip!

Blessings! Colin On behalf of the VCHSC Junior Class
Posted by Colin Mansfield at 10:12 AM 1 comment:
Saturday, February 21, 2009

Landed safely in chicago. Bad weather, doesn't look bad enough for delay though. Check http://WWIIhelmet.blog-spot.com
Posted by Colin Mansfield at 5:01 PM No comments:

Oh, btw our plane leaves today at about 5 today. Just to keep ya in the loop :)
Posted by Colin Mansfield at 10:23 AM No comments:

West Point, etc.

Went to bed at about 3am last night. Great day yester-
day! This morning we split into three groups. Kevin and
Brian Egizi along with myself and my dad went to visit
USMA at West Point, the college Brian and I would like
to attend. Another group went into New Haven to check
out Yale, while a third group decided it would be in their
best interest/health to sleep in.

West Point was awesome; hopefully I'll be able to get
some pics on later.

More updates to come on http://twitter.com/WWII-
helmetColin

Posted by Colin Mansfield at 10:20 AM

Friday, February 20, 2009
Friday In Its Entirety

Wow! What an amazing day! And so jam packed!
The day started with quick showers all around, then off
to Middletown. Our good friend, Sara Elander tagged
along all through today as well. Once in Middletown,
we ate at the Athenian II diner for some fantastic break-
fast. Letting my food digest, I plugged in the coordinates
to our much awaited and planned for destination: the
house of A.J. Malone.

The anticipation hung in the air like a thick fog; every-
one knew the importance of today.

As we pulled up to the Malone house (easily identified
by the 15 cars parked out front) I immediately noticed the
local NBC affiliate, channel 30 truck parked out front; to
top it off, a cameraman got footage of us rolling up.

The proceedings went amazing, better then planned.
Mrs. Malone was so very kind and gracious, and her
family was extraordinary! Our class brought various

gifts... Gold, frankincense, and myrrh... Ok just kidding! Mr. Mansfield, my dad, had portraits made of the helmet that we presented to the Malone family. Also, our class presented Bibles which each of us had signed. Finally, the time had come.

With much enthusiasm, Mr. Mansfield reached into the bag behind him, and brought forth the item of most interest: A.J. Malone's helmet. The cameras flashed, the film whirled, and the faces grinned. Speaking on behalf of my class, the moment was everything we could have hoped for and more. Mr. Mansfield handed the helmet to Mrs. Malone, and with a few more words the procession was over. We stayed at the house for about another hour and a half in community with the family and friends of the Malone's, as well as doing a few press interviews.

After the main event, our class was given the honor of visiting Mr. Malone's grave site with his daughter, Lorraine Decker. Truly a touching experience. My dad said a few words, and Austin prayed.

Then, it was off to New York!

Realize that originally, we hadn't planned on going to NY. It wasn't until Boston, yesterday, that Shalom suggested it. Great idea!

Anyways, we started our NY tour by hitting up the ferry. Once on there, we were able to take pics of the Statue of Liberty. Very fun!

From the ferry we went to ground zero (pic on below post) then we were off to Grand Central Station (pic below as well). After eating at GCS, we headed back to our cars, did a quick drive by of time square, then started the 2 hour process of getting home.

Now, as I sit here blogging from my dads iPhone, I look back on today with skepticism. Is it really possible we did all this in one day? The answer is yes, and my tired feet remind me of that fact.

Who knows what tomorrow holds before we head home at 5ish!

Colin
Posted with LifeCast

Acknowledgements

"My sincere thanks go out to the following people for helping us in Finding Malone:

- My father and friend of 18 years, Bill Mansfield, for receiving my tribute and returning the honor to me.
- A. J. (Tony) Malone, for his service to the nation during WWII, as well as in loving his wife and raising his family. We never met, but I carried a part of you around with me for almost 40 years.
- The family of Tony Malone – thank you *one and all* for your being available to receive a bunch of Idaho students into your Connecticut home for that marvelous day of returning the helmet.
- The high school students of the Vineyard Christian Home School Co-op in Boise, Idaho, without whose able research A.J. Malone's helmet would have simply stayed in my family's possession: Austin Townend, Caleb Grad, Jared Mercer, Drew Zimmerman, Mary Zimmerman, Brian Egizi, Shalom Knight, Sara Hardy, Lanae Langdon, Hannah Freeman, Skylar Harris, Michael Page and Colin Mansfield

- Former Member of the U.S. House of Representatives, Walt Minnick, for his visionary kindness in helping supply the air transportation for the students.
- John Foster, former Chief of Staff to Congressman Walt Minnick, for helping me with the details of getting the class from Idaho to Connecticut.
- Carole Cloyd of US Airways, for seeing the true beauty of honoring a soldier from WWII. Without you and former-Congressman Minnick we would never have walked into the Malone family's life.
- Tri Robinson and Trevor Estes of VineyardBoise for seeing the big picture of a small helmet. You didn't know what you were getting when you asked me to take over as Principal, did you?
- The parents who supported this effort and those who joined us on the trip – you were such a blessing to all of us.
- My son, Colin Mansfield – for showing me honor throughout this overall project – the trip *and* the book. May the example of SGT. A. J. Malone and CMSGT William E. Mansfield light your way as a US Army officer.
- My daughter, Meg, for her calligraphy skills when she was 11 and as an adult, for supporting her own military serviceman, Caleb Roe, US Air Force and for loving me.
- My bride, Susan, for calling my attention *for the first time* to a name written on the inside of a WWI era helmet – a name that had been in front of my eyes for almost 40 years. Thank you for encouraging that I write this amazing story, for

helping me find myself and my father in 1995, and for joining us in finding Malone."

- My Irish mother, Virginia Agnes Maguire Mansfield who taught me to laugh, love and be mischievous. I learned well.
- My stepmother, Marilyn Mansfield, who faithfully loved my father till the end and received his love back. He loved you so much.
- My Irish Grand Pop, John Joseph Maguire, who was the most unique man in my childhood world. He influenced me to be strong, humorous, direct and always know how to use illusion. The quarter out of the ear was merely one trick...
- My Uncle Richard (Dick) Maguire, whose help in reviewing the Philadelphia portion of the story was so very helpful.
- My oldest sister, Kathy, for vetting the manuscript and using her first-born instincts and memory to make it accurate and real. Love ya, Kath.
- My brothers and sisters, Kathy, Gary, Janet, JoAnne, Joyce and Ken – for thriving and surviving together with me during our childhood. You are the best Band of Brothers and Sisters that a warrior could ever have the honor of loving *and* liking.
- My stepsisters Diane and Cheri for your friendship and love all these many years. You were grafted into the family tree and you flourished well. Thanks for loving Dad.
- To Paul Ruth, for showing Grandma and Grandpa the love of Christ by serving them everyday and every night. I am so glad you are my friend.

- Wayne McKamie and Paul Nobrega (http://focusseminar.com/ and http://empowerboise.com/) for their impact in helping me grow in my healing with my Dad, even after the events of this book.
- To Robert Sweesy for the visionary boldness of starting Endurance Press, allowing me to peer in, every so often. Gambling on me was much appreciated.
- To my agent, Chris Ferebee of Chris Ferebee and Associates for the lunch with our wives and Larry Kelly on Catalina Island and for the subsequent hard talk afterwards. Thanks for being my literary thug; *now* it can be said, "nice book."

And to:

- Dennis Rainey, for writing *The Tribute*. You changed the lives and friendship of two men named Mansfield, a family connected to them and all their grandchildren. Thank you for teaching many of us to pay tribute to those who may not have honored us. You are indeed, Dennis, The Greater!

CPSIA information can be obtained at www.ICGtesting.com
Printed in the USA
LVOW01s1405270515

440100LV00017B/117/P